Managing the Multinational Subsidiary

James M. Hulbert and William K. Brandt

COLUMBIA UNIVERSITY

Holt Rinehart and Winston

NEW YORK   CHICAGO   SAN FRANCISCO   DALLAS
TORONTO   MONTREAL

Holt Business Success Series

Dedicated to the
Memory of Our
Fathers
Alfred G. Hulbert
Karl W. Brandt

Library of Congress Cataloging in Publication Data

Hulbert, James M
   Managing the multinational subsidiary.

   (Holt business success series)
   Includes index.
   1. Subsidiary corporations—Management. 2. International business enterprises—Management. 3. Com-
parative management. I. Brandt, William K., joint
author. II. Title. III. Series.
HD62.3.H84   658.1'8   80-23924
ISBN: 0-03-057436-6

Foreword

This is a remarkable work, not because it is for or against any one particular point of view, but because it adds a new dimension to the study of the multinational corporation. Messrs J. M. Hulbert and W. K. Brandt examine the MNC from the point of view of its subsidiary, with in-depth analysis of the different modes of operation within one particular country.

I have tried for years to convince various audiences that one could not speak of MNCs in general, as if they were all alike. In fact, they differ greatly from one another, because they belong to different industries, have their origins in different countries and cultures, and follow different policies and practices. The failure to recognize these disparities is at the root of many of the difficulties one finds today in writing codes of conduct and other forms of guidance for multinational companies.

The authors make clear these differences, comparing and contrasting the different styles of management found among European, American, and Japanese multinationals and the historical and other reasons for them. What might be added is that if the subsidiaries have different behavior as a function of the nationality of the head office, the head offices themselves also behave very differently from one another. The permutations are very complex.

Given these disparities, the striking thing is the ability of the multinational to draw together people from so many different backgrounds and cultures to work together on common tasks. One of the keys, I believe, is to be found in the planning process. In my experience, that process requires the definition of objectives at local, national, and international levels, and then the coordination of those plans into a logical whole. At the international headquarters level, I never cease to be impressed by the ability of people of as many as 30 different nationalities with many different languages and cultures to discover the common ground that can unite them in cooperative action. Planning is a remarkable tool for giving people at many different levels a chance to participate in the decision-making process and to have a stake in the progress of their company at all levels.

Communication, of course, is the key. Good communication is not just a matter of a common language, but a convergence of ideas and goals. It is also a matter of choosing the best person for the job, regardless of nationality, and then ensuring that that person is exposed to a variety of learning experiences, nationally and internationally. The goal is to equip him or her to evaluate and weigh the trade-offs which confront us all, in one way or another, in this world of increasing complexity and interdependence. For me, the development of a corps of executives who have a deep understanding of world problems may be the condition of success of the MNC.

On a larger scale, the book brings into focus one of the basic challenges of our age — the challenge to cooperate on an international basis. For the challenge faced by the multinational and its subsidiaries is mirrored in many of the human dilemmas facing our world in the last two decades of this century.

It may be helpful, in this context, to remind ourselves that tensions and conflicts are not necessarily aberrations, but to a large extent part of the natural order. We find in physics the concept that "for every action, there is an equal and opposite reaction"; in government, the concept of "checks and balances"; in law, the adversary system; in society at large, what has been called "countervailing power".

Whether such tension is constructive or destructive is largely a question of whether and how it can be reconciled — and most of the institutions and procedures of civilized society are, in fact, designed to reconcile that tension towards desirable ends.

This book underlines the myriad ways in which that reconciliation has to take place, on a day-to-day basis, in the multinational company — centralization versus decentralization; international coordination versus local responsibility; "bottom-up" versus "top-down" planning; powers reserved to the head office versus powers delegated. The business of the multinational corporation is, in part, the management of such differences towards constructive ends.

In this sense, the multinational manager, the student of multinationals, and the informed citizen are all in a position to benefit from this excellent book, and to extrapolate from it an idea of what the future can be.

Jacques Maisonrouge
President, IBM Europe
May 7, 1980

Preface

Since World War II, geographical expansion into foreign markets through exports or direct manufacturing has served as a principal avenue for growth for most large corporations. Managing the foreign operations which result, be they sales branches or wholly-owned subsidiaries, has often caused severe pains and strains within executive ranks. How alike or different these operations are from domestic affiliates and how they should be treated is not well understood even in the most experienced multinationals. The quest continues, therefore, for "the better way" to deal with the foreign subsidiary.

The book addresses some of the more common managerial problems faced by managers at home office and at the foreign subsidiary. It deals with questions about:

- organizational structure between home office and subsidiary
- how plans are developed and adopted within the subsidiary and the problems inherent in the process
- choice of subsidiary strategies and the programs designed to implement them
- communicating between home office and the subsidiary
- controls used by home office to keep subsidiary managers on track

Three features set this book apart from other writings dealing with these issues. First, the foreign subsidiary is the principal focus of our efforts. Without becoming advocates for subsidiary managers, we study the institutions and problems primarily from their perspective. Second, the book compares the management practices for the three nationality groups responsible for a major portion of world business today: the North Americans, the Western Europeans, and the Japanese. Third, the practices discussed and recommendations presented are based on extensive research through personal interviews with subsidiary executives, as well as the usual review of academic and management literature.

The book is presented with three audiences in mind. For the manager involved in foreign operations, at home office or abroad, the book should help to explain why certain problems arise, how other companies (perhaps competitors) address them, and what might be done to overcome the difficulties. Thus, in addition to describing the issues, of which most managers are already well aware, the book offers explanations and recommendations for change.

For the student wanting to understand better how multinationals operate, the book provides a rather thorough investigation of their activities and problems. For classroom use with basic courses in international business, it is best used in conjunction with a more general text on multinational operations.

Researchers should find the book useful in developing hypotheses about multinational operations or about differences based on national origin of the firm. The research on which the book is based raises many issues demanding further study.

Since this book must meet the needs of several different audiences, we have tried to organize it in such a way as to meet their different interests. Accordingly, the body of the text, while it refers to research findings, is written in a non-technical manner and should present little difficulty to the professional manager or average student. For more advanced students, as well as the researcher, we have incorporated several appendices dealing with more technical aspects of the research which underlies the book.

To complete a project of this magnitude is somewhat analogous to producing a movie. Behind the actors seen on the screen there are numerous directors, technicians, financiers, and support staff. This publication was likewise dependent on many persons and to each one we express our sincere gratitude.

This book is one of a series of publications resulting from the Columbia University Multinational Enterprise Project, supported by the Ford Foundation and the Graduate School of Business of Columbia University.

The most vital contribution, in the form of information, was given by the 125 executives who responded patiently for hours on end to our questions. In this book the executives' names and their companies remain anonymous, but their individual contributions to our work are very personal and valued.

Our colleagues at Columbia University contributed many comments, critical and stimulating, during the course of our study and we extend our sincere appreciation to each of them.

In Brazil, our godfather in this study was Professor Raimar Richers of the Fundacao Getulio Vargas, who encouraged and assisted our efforts from the beginning.

To the many research assistants and secretaries who participated along the way we are indeed grateful. One who stood by us from start to finish, typing endless numbers of "final drafts," was Harriet Leonard and to her we extend a special thank you.

To everyone who supported and contributed to this research and publication we are truly indebted. At the same time we bear the responsibility for errors of omission or commission found in this work.

New York   J. M. Hulbert
June 1980   W. K. Brandt

Contents

Chapter 1

Introduction

$\mathbf{T}$he multinational corporation, assailed by some and praised by others, is destined to remain a focus of public attention. On the one hand, it is viewed as a paragon of economic virtue, facilitating efficient resource allocation by its ability to transcend national boundaries; on the other hand, it is condemned as an economic imperialist, in some respects worse than the outright colonialist.

Yet despite its preeminence in the corporate world, surprisingly little is known about how the multinational company works. Although a number of good studies are available, these are outnumbered by polemics, many of which reflect the authors' prejudices but contain little factual information. Further, many of the studies deal with such issues as the macro- or microeconomic role of multinationals, their policies with respect to host governments, or their role in economic development. A few deal with management issues, but they focus on the headquarters role. This book, however, is concerned with the management of subsidiaries, where so many international managers are blooded (and bloodied!) without the benefit of formal background or training in the particular problems and challenges presented by subsidiary management. We make a modest attempt to redress the imbalance in the literature by offering to managers, researchers, and policymakers not only empirical findings about subsidiary management practices, but also some specific guidelines and suggestions for the improvement of those practices. We hope that at the very least some managers may thereby avoid the chronic problems which recur with monotonous frequency in the absence of any sharing of experience.

The Multinational: The Eye of the Storm

The men who run the global corporations are the first in history with the organization, technology, money, and ideology to make a credible try at managing the world as an integrated unit.[1]

Since World War II the world economy has undergone a transformation as dramatic in its impact as the shock waves of the Industrial Revolution. The merchants of change in this latest revolution are a handful of corporations, fewer than a thousand, which came to realize that "for business purposes the boundaries that separate one nation from another are no more real than the equator."[2] They viewed the world outside their home country not as scattered customers but as an extension of a single market.

For manufacturing firms, the initial extensions represented lateral moves from one developed nation to another — from the United States to Western Europe or vice versa — whereas the more recent movements have focused on the developing, or Third World, markets. As the markets of Western Europe and the United States have matured and grown more competitive, developing and less developed countries have become increasingly attractive to multinational corporations, whose desire for growth seems unabated.

As a result of their growth and omnipresence, multinationals have come to occupy an increasingly important position in the economic, political, and social spheres of the contemporary world. They have thereby become extremely visible and vulnerable targets for attack and invectives in home and host countries and in political, academic, literary, and journalistic quarters. Sir Ronald Edwards has recently stated that multinationals now occupy for

[1]Richard J. Barnet and Ronald E. Muller, *Global Reach* (New York: Simon and Schuster, 1974), p. 13.

[2]Jacques G. Maisonrouge, "How International Business Can Further World Understanding." Speech delivered September 16, 1971. In recent personal correspondence M. Maisonrouge reaffirmed his belief that the "desire to improve the human condition transcends the boundaries that separate one nation from another."

many people "a place roughly equivalent to that of Satan in medieval times."[3]

Critics in the home countries of multinational companies charge them with robbing workers of jobs by moving plants overseas, exploiting the raw materials and the peoples of poor nations, and endangering peace by corrupting foreign governments. Some economists criticize the companies for their pricing practices, suggesting that multinational corporations are cartelizing the world economy and fouling the adjustment processes of the monetary system. Others claim that no company can be truly international in the sense that it either has no allegiance to any nation-state or has equal allegiance toward all nations in which it operates. Because the multinationals are almost exclusively controlled by interests in the developed world, critics charge that they represent another form of imperialistic domination. Reflecting the same concern, the United Nations group on multinationals reports:

The divergence in objectives between nation-states and multinational corporations, compounded by social and cultural factors, often creates tensions. Multinational corporations, through a variety of options available to them, can encroach at times upon national sovereignty by undermining the ability of nation-states to pursue their national and international objectives. Moreover, there are conflicts of interest regarding participation in decision-making and the equitable division of benefits between multinational corporations and host as well as home countries. In recent years the situation has been sharpened, on the one hand by changes in the internal socio-political conditions of many countries, and on the other, by shifts in bargaining positions. As a result, existing arrangements are frequently questioned and new ones are sought.[4]

The multinationals are not defenseless in these verbal jousts. The so-called optimists see the multinational as the most powerful engine of economic progress so far developed by man. Referring to the positive role played by multinationals, IBM's Jacques G. Maisonrouge has noted: "They have become agents of change

---

[3]Quoted in a speech by David Rockefeller, "World Needs Free Business Climate," at the University of Manchester, England, as reported in the *Los Angeles Times,* May 11, 1975.

[4]*Multinational Corporations in World Development* (New York: Department of Economic and Social Affairs, ST/ECA/190, United Nations, 1973); cited in *The Frightening Angels: A Study of U.S. Multinationals in Developing Nations,* by Anant R. Negandi and S. Benjamin Prasad (Kent, Ohio: The Kent State University Press, 1975).

and progress, for they are building what, to all intents and purposes, must be considered a new world economic system — one in which the constraints of geography have yielded to the logic of efficiency."[5] In support of this view, Donald M. Kendall, chairman and chief executive officer of Pepsico Inc. has echoed: ". . . from this conception of the world as a single system will come a richer, and far more rewarding life for us all — not simply as Americans, but as human beings."[6]

Nor are defenders exclusively businessmen. Some economists argue that multinational firms help to correct market imperfections and increase the validity of traditional economic theory. Others point to the transfer of technology, capital, and management skills to Third World nations and to the expansion of jobs and real wealth in home and host-country markets. The internationalists stress the cause of world peace, which is supposedly enhanced by stronger economic bonds. They also suggest that at a time when people are losing faith in governments, the multinational corporations boast an impressive record of efficiency and progress. Professor Neil H. Jacoby, for example, argues that the multinational "is, beyond doubt, the most powerful agency for global and economic unity that our century has produced."[7] Supporting this view, the eminent historian Arnold Toynbee argues that multinational corporations bridge the gap "between economic systems,"[8] which, given the "immense resistance to anything like a world government,"[9] makes them a necessity. Professor Emile Benoit, of Columbia University, has argued:

The MNC may be viewed as a powerful engine for diffusing the benefits of superior management and technology across national boundaries thereby improving the world's allocation of resources and taking fuller advantage of the economies of scale . . . . Contrary to what many suppose, there is no fundamental clash between the MNC and the host government. Indeed, the MNC can contribute notably to host country na-

---

[5]Quoted by Donald M. Kendall, "The Need for the Multinational Corporation," in John K. Ryans (ed.), *The Multinational Business World of the 1930's* (Kent, Ohio: Center for Business and Economic Research, Kent State University, 1974), p. 22; cited in *The Frightening Angels,* p. 5.
[6]Kendall, *ibid.,* p. 23; cited in *The Frightening Angels,* p. 6.
[7]Neil H. Jacoby, "The Multinational Corporation," *The Center Magazine,* Vol. III (May 1970), pp. 37–55, at p. 54.
[8]Arnold Toynbee, "As I See It," *Forbes,* April 15, 1974, pp. 68–70.
[9]*Ibid.*

tional objectives, given adequate encouragement and sensible controls . . . .[10]

These intensive dialogues, arguments, and counterarguments are further complicated by inconclusive research results on the issues. Studies to determine the multinational impact on balance of payments, national economies, trade, employment, and other topics have generally yielded weak or conflicting results. Despite further attempts to measure impacts, the United Nations report offers the following warning:

The complexity of the subject and the controversy that surrounds it call for serious analysis lest myths should prove more appealing than facts and emotions stronger than reason . . . . The basic facts and issues still need to be disentangled from the mass of opinion and ideology and a practical programme of action still awaits formulation.[11]

These conclusions differ little from our opening comments. Yet the brief review of conflicting viewpoints highlights the fact that any young man or woman contemplating a career in international management is stepping into a seething cauldron of political and economic controversy. Nor do we expect this situation to change greatly, at least within the next five or ten years.

Managing the Multinational Company: Two Perspectives

Clearly, there are as many perspectives on multinational companies, and what should be their objectives, strategies, and procedures, as there are interested commentators. However, our intent is to focus on one of these perspectives, that of the subsidiary. First, we should review and contrast this perspective with the other key management perspective on the multinational — that of home office. Although the home office has more of a "top down" viewpoint, whereas the subsidiary is more "bottom up," both parties should share a common interest in the progress of the company as a whole. Their different roles, however, mean that their perspectives are, in fact, quite different. Further, within each or-

---

[10]Emile Benoit, "The Attack on the Multinationals," *Columbia Journal of World Business,* November–December 1972, p. 22.
[11]*Multinational Corporations in World Development* (New York: Department of Economic and Social Affairs, ST/ECA/190, United Nations, 1973), as quoted in *The Frightening Angels,* p. 16.

ganizational unit, subsidiary or home office, there is also divergence of perspective and objective, resulting from the different backgrounds and experiences of managers, as well as the sometimes conflicting demands of their current positions.

Recognizing, then, that our dichotomy is oversimplified, we shall nonetheless pursue our discussion within this context, because it has proved to be a very fruitful means of gaining insight into the operational and organizational problems posed by multinationals.[12] The home office, of course, is faced with the immense task of attempting to coordinate the operations of the company's many subsidiaries (including its domestic activities) in such a way that the company as a whole succeeds in furthering its objectives. As we discuss at length (particularly in Chapters 2 and 6), there are many possible approaches to organizing and operating in order to achieve international integration, but the label "multinational" must imply a higher degree of coordination than exists in a holding company context, where any benefits of international operations must be restricted to portfolio diversification of financial risk.

Consequently, to a greater or lesser extent, the home office must attempt to extend some control over the activities of its subsidiaries, whether that control is restricted to the approval of capital expenditure requests of $5 million or more, or is extended to require home office approval of expenditures of a few hundred dollars and insistence on common branding, packaging, and advertising. Both the degree of control and the attitudes of home office personnel in exercising control are important influences on the organizational climate that evolves.

The situation at the subsidiary level is different. Though by no means diametrically opposed to the home office goals, the objectives of the subsidiary manager are necessarily somewhat divergent. First, home office decisions that may ultimately be advantageous to the company as a whole may have unfortunate implications for the individual subsidiaries. Where subsidiary top management is dominated by home country personnel, many conflicts can occur, but even when subsidiary management is heavily staffed by nationals of the host country it is easy to see

[12]Further work, now in progress, confirms this viewpoint. See William G. Egelhoff, William K. Brandt, and William H. Newman, "Organizational Design in Multinational Corporations." Research Working Paper No. 241A, Columbia University Graduate School of Business, 1979.

how conflicts of loyalty arise. Most subsidiary managers are, of course, competing for promotion, yet the subsidiary operating results often used in developing "league tables" for promotability are rarely adjusted to reflect the impact of uncontrollable factors on performance. The extent to which an individual subsidiary's results are hurt or bettered by decisions taken for the common good is, of course, often extremely difficult, if not impossible, to measure. The customary response of avoiding any attempt at formal adjustment, however, in turn endows with false and often highly political impact the figures that are used.

The foregoing is not meant to imply that adversarial elements in the subsidiary/home office relationship are necessarily harmful. Some companies, such as General Motors, foster a degree of internal competition which may be beneficial. However, the discussion does, we hope, make the point that there is an inherent difference in perspective between subsidiary and home office. Whereas the viewpoint of the latter is commonly adopted by writers and researchers dealing with the multinational, few have approached its management problems from the perspective of the subsidiary. This is our intent.

SCOPE AND STRUCTURE OF THE BOOK

Two major objectives were established for this book: descriptive and prescriptive. First, we aim to describe formally the management practices of multinational subsidiaries, contrasting the approaches of European, North American, and Japanese companies. Second, from a sound basis of descriptive understanding, we develop recommendations directed toward improving the ways in which multinational subsidiaries are managed.

To meet the above objectives, the book draws heavily on our survey of sixty-three multinational subsidiaries operating in Brazil. The results of the survey, reported in detail elsewhere,[13] provide the empirical basis for much of the positive and normative content of the book. We have also drawn on a variety of other sources,

---

[13]The full study is reported in William K. Brandt and James M. Hulbert, *A Empresa Multinacional no Brazil: Un Estudo Empirico,* Rio: Zahar Editores, 1977. Appendix D to this book describes the methodology of the study, containing descriptions of the companies and the managers included in the study.

including our experiences while working in consulting or executive development capacities.

The book is directed primarily to managers, public officials, and those in the academic and professional worlds who have an interest in the operation of the multinational corporation. Business executives will not find in it a source of competitive tips, since no companies are identified. They should, however, find it interesting for its description and appraisal of alternative approaches to organization, management, and strategy, as well as for changes that might be forthcoming. For students of international management the book represents an overview of management practices in major multinational subsidiaries, with particular interest for those who have followed the development of the Brazilian economy. To our knowledge, there is no other book available which focuses on subsidiary problems, and we hope that this text will prove helpful to those concerned with these management issues.

We start with a discussion of the organizational issues involved in multinational operations. As we note in the first part of Chapter 2, many firms have followed a similar path in the evolution of their organization structures. Nonetheless, at a given point in time, we find a variety of organizational forms represented; in the second part of the chapter we examine some of the factors responsible for this variety. Just as the organization structure relating home office to its subsidiaries shows variation, so of course does the structure of subsidiaries themselves. We discuss these differences too, with specific reference to our Brazilian findings, before considering some guidelines in developing organization structure. As in other studies, we find significant performance differences among contrasting organization structures, but it would be premature to ascribe these differences solely to organizational factors.

Chapter 3 is concerned with the planning process, focusing at first primarily on planning within the subsidiary. We note that many of the planning problems observed domestically occur also in subsidiaries, but the complications created by multinational operations seem to magnify considerably the impact of these problems. Although we attempt to classify and analyze some of the problems we have observed, the very interactive and participative nature of the planning process itself makes cause and effect difficult to untangle.

Strategy formulation provides the subject matter for Chapter 4. We look briefly at the objectives and strategies of the subsidiaries included in our survey, but soon focus on one of the key bones of contention in many multinationals, namely: What should be the role of headquarters in establishing strategy for the subsidiary? Our empirical findings suggest that the home office/subsidiary relationship in strategy formulation is more complex than many have assumed, and this would seem to be a fruitful area for more work. We also review some performance results in Chapter 4, although for researchers, as for management, assessing the "true" performance of a multinational is by no means easy.

Chapter 5 is devoted to the subject of communications between subsidiary and home office. We look at various forms of personal and impersonal communications and their perceived effect. We also develop some ideas for the better management of intracompany communications, a crucial function in a multinational company.

Chapter 6 is devoted to the complex and controversial subject of headquarters control of subsidiary activities. We have adopted a broad and strategic approach to control, a perspective consistent with contemporary views of the process and one that facilitates dealing with the associated issues of organization structure and its evolution. We also examine control practices within a narrower, more budgetary framework, and complete the discussion by presenting some key design issues for the control system.

Our concluding chapter integrates our findings around profiles of European, American, and Japanese multinationals. We then discuss how we expect these profiles to change as the multinational company evolves, our results suggesting that a convergence of structure and style is likely to accompany increasingly global perspectives. We also review the situation with respect to the multinational and the developing world. Although the issues involved in this debate are too complex and multifarious to be resolved in this book, we find grounds for anticipating new forms of modus vivendi in the future.

Finally, Appendices A–D delve into some of our findings in more detail. Appendix A concentrates on the research results for organization structure. The focus of Appendix B is the formulation of subsidiary strategy. In Appendix C we present our findings on patterns of communication flow among home office and subsidiaries. For those interested in methodology, Appendix D describes the Brazilian survey of multinational subsidiaries, and gives profiles of both the executives interviewed and the companies they managed.

Chapter 2

Organizing for Multinational Operations

Organizational structure provides the legal managerial link between the headquarters of a multinational enterprise and its foreign affiliates. In its managerial role the structure becomes the formal framework for facilitating and guiding decision making of widely diverse functions, geographical regions, markets, and product groups. Design of the structure helps to identify where different decisions are made, communication needs and flows between managers, and the forms of support and control required at each level of the organization.

The rapid development of trade and manufacturing outside domestic markets has seriously strained the organizational linkages of most firms. Whereas traditional structures frequently resulted from historical accidents, technical needs, personal preferences, and perhaps a theory of organization, the evolution of an international strategy has demanded more effective and generally more complex structures.

The array of organizational structures adopted by multinational firms has been described and reported in great detail elsewhere.[1]

[1] John M. Stopford and Louis T. Wells, Jr., *Managing the Multinational Enterprise* (New York: Basic Books, 1972), pp. 9–29. Michael Z. Brooke and H. Lee Remmers, *The Strategy of Multinational Enterprise* (New York: American Elsevier Publishers, 1970), pp. 25–63. Richard D. Robinson, *International Business Management* (New York: Holt, Rinehart and Winston, 1973), pp. 585–619. Stefan H. Robock, Kenneth Simmonds, and Jack Zwick, *International Business and Multinational Enterprise*, rev. ed. (Homewood, Ill.: Richard D. Irwin, 1977), pp. 427–50. Lawrence G. Franko, *The European Multinationals* (Stamford, Conn.:

Our objective in this chapter is to explore:

- The forces and trends which underlie the shift from one structure to another.
- The characteristics of the parent company and its subsidiary associated with structural changes.
- Alternative ways to reduce organizational problems.
- The relationship between structure and the company's performance.

Since, by definition, multinational firms are already involved in foreign markets, we devote little attention to the initial move abroad. The immediate problem faced by firms in our survey concerned ways to modify and redesign the existing international structure. After examining the characteristics and conditions associated with different structures and their possible effects on performance, suggestions for improvement emerge. We begin with a description of the broad structural forms common to most multinational firms.

FOREIGN EXPANSION AND STRUCTURAL CHANGE

Despite the claim of most managers that "his or her organization is unique," the evolution of structure as firms become more involved abroad has followed surprisingly similar patterns.[2] Whether by design or default, firms with few foreign subsidiaries generally operated with looser or more personal linkages between headquarters and foreign operations. During this initial period a direct-reporting structure was frequently used. The subsidiary manager reported directly to the chief or other top executive of the parent company. Supervision, counsel, and evaluation were conducted on a personal basis between these two executives, both of whom typically operated without the support of large staff groups.

With the growth of foreign sales and operations, the international component of the firm demanded increasing time and attention. In many North American and Japanese firms particularly, the chief executives delegated responsibilities to a small cadre of managers accountable for foreign activities. The international division,

Greylock, 1976), pp. 186–212. M. Y. Yoshino, *Japan's Multinational Enterprises* (Cambridge, Mass.: Harvard University Press, 1976), pp. 127–42.
[2]Stanley M. Davis, "Trends in the Organization of Multinational Corporations," *Columbia Journal of World Business,* Vol. 18, (Summer 1976), pp. 59–71.

as it is commonly labeled, was designed to form an umbrella over the firm's foreign business.

Variations of this structure abounded as firms attempted cosmetic changes to overcome inherent weaknesses of the international division structure. A common move was to add another layer to the organizational hierarchy by creating regional offices to focus on the firm's business in a specific geographic area. Other companies established product groups within the international division in an effort to provide more technical and marketing support to the subsidiary.

As an international division grows in size and importance, however, the same forces that led to its creation encourage its demise. The need for improved coordination and integration between domestic and foreign operations requires a structure that encourages a worldwide perspective by managers at home and abroad. Top management, for example, begins to recognize the benefits that might accrue from coordinated production on a regional or worldwide scale. Subsidiary managers become aware that their products are part of a production and marketing strategy extending well beyond local markets.

To achieve this worldwide perspective many firms have adopted some form of global structure. Four designs emerged during the 1960s to replace the international division. Firms that based their strategic decisions around products or product groups assigned worldwide responsibilities to product divisions. Others separated the worldwide organization into several regional groups, each with total responsibility for all activities in its geographic area. A few firms — for example, the oil companies and some European companies — structured their activities around functional duties such as production, marketing, and finance. Still others chose a combination of two or three forms, sometimes giving them coequal responsibility in a matrix design. A recent trend in some firms is moving away from an area or product structure to a market orientation which groups countries on the basis of market homogeneity instead of geographic or product proximity.

In the sixty-three corporations we surveyed, the following structures were identified:

Direct reporting	18%
International division	48%
Global structure	34%
	100%

The Chain of Command

The choice of one organization structure over another involves much more than mental perspective or the rearrangement of tasks and people. One very visible distinction in design is the "height" versus "flatness" of the formal hierarchy — that is, the number of levels in the organizational hierarchy between the foreign subsidiary manager and the chief operating executive of the parent company.[3] This measure is often labeled "vertical span," since it deals with the relationships up and down the hierarchy. Among the firms interviewed, the vertical span ranged from zero to four, with an average of 1.76 levels between the chief executives at the subsidiary and at the parent company.

The relation between vertical span and the general form of structure is reported in Table 1. Firms with international divisions maintained the tallest hierarchies, with an average of 2.44 levels. Global structures operated with an average of 1.61 levels, and most direct-reporting structures by definition had no organizational levels between the two executives. In a few cases the subsidiary manager reported through a second-level executive, but the structure retained the character of a direct-reporting system.

Table 1

Vertical Span and Structural Design of Organizations

	Vertical Span[a]							Proportion of Firms (percent)
Structural Design	0	1	2	3	4	Total (percent)	Mean	
Direct reporting	80%	20%	0%	0%	0%	100%	0.20	18%
International division	0	11	48	26	15	100	2.44	48
Global structure	0	61	22	11	6	100	1.61	34
Total	15%	29%	31%	16%	9%	100%	1.76	100%

[a]*Vertical span represents the number of levels in formal organization hierarchy between chief operating executive of the parent company and its foreign subsidiary.*

[3]Because the titles such as chairman, president, and country manager often belie the locus of true decision-making authority, special efforts were made to identify the actual chief operating officer at both levels.

The results shown in Table 1 are consistent with the evolutionary pattern described earlier. For most firms the growth of foreign and often domestic business required a shift away from a direct-reporting structure in which the chief executive had retained a personal tie to the individual subsidiaries. The international division which followed the direct-reporting structure worked well in the beginning in many firms, particularly where technology was more standard and product lines were narrow. With the growth in size and complexity, however, headquarters responded by adding more levels to the hierarchy, sometimes to the point where four layers of line management interceded between the chief executive of the subsidiary and the chief executive of the parent company. Each layer offered a short-term remedy, but with continued growth abroad and the inevitable transition to a worldwide perspective, the additional layers hindered effective decision making. The global structure was designed to overcome some of these limitations, partly by eliminating levels in the vertical hierarchy. This structure generally leads to more comprehensive planning and control systems, while simultaneously allowing more direct relationships between headquarters and subsidiary executives.

DETERMINANTS OF ORGANIZATION STRUCTURE

Few multinational firms have followed the evolutionary path in the step-by-step sequence outlined above. Many move from direct reporting to an international division, but no further. Some shift from direct reporting to global structures, without the intervening stage of international division. Still others continue to report directly, with no immediate plans for change. This section explores the reasons behind these choices by considering the characteristics of the parent company and its foreign subsidiaries that might influence structure.

Nationality of Parent Company

The first set of factors refers to the national origin of the parent corporation. To what extent does being a European, a Japanese, or a North American firm influence the type of organization structure adopted? To answer this question we must review some historical and cultural antecedents that have helped to shape the structures used today.

European Organizations. In the archetypal European company, key decisions were typically made at the top by a small group of managers who, in one author's words, "were relatively free to behave in the tradition of the merchant trader."[4] Culture and history provide some of the answers behind the highly centralized and functionally oriented structures observed in the classic European firm.[5] Throughout their early history, European firms maintained highly personal relations with their foreign affiliates. In the nineteenth century, family members were appointed to head the subsidiaries.[6] Although this practice has given way to fewer family ties, in many European firms personal relationships still provide the principal bond between headquarters and its foreign operations.

Following World War II Europe was a seller's market, a condition not conducive to major changes or long-term thinking. Market planning was regarded with skepticism at best, antipathy at worst.[7] Europe's history of cartelization reinforced the tendency to deemphasize planning and management controls. These economic conditions, combined with cultural values which encouraged concentration of management authority, were major reasons for the lean-looking structure of traditional European firms.

Many of the European companies in our survey fit the classic structure even today. Reflecting their preference for centralized

[4]John M. Stopford, "Organizing the Multinational Firm: Can the Americans Learn from the Europeans?" in Michael Brooke and H. Lee Remmers (eds.), *The Multinational Company in Europe* (Ann Arbor: The University of Michigan Press, 1972), p. 87.

[5]Reference to a "classic European firm" is made with caution, recognizing that generalizations across Continental and British enterprises are tentative at best. Preliminary analyses of our data and the conclusions of Franko, however, support our contention that European firms as a group behaved distinctly differently from Japanese or North American firms and can be analyzed as a group without serious bias. See Lawrence G. Franko, "The Move Toward a Multinational Structure in European Organizations," *Administrative Science Quarterly* Vol. 19, (1974), pp. 493–506.

[6]Franko, *ibid.*

[7]John U. Farley, James M. Hulbert, and David Weinstein, "Marketing Planning Systems in European Multi-market Industrial Companies," paper presented at the July 1975 meeting of the Academy of International Business, Fontainebleau, France.

decision making and a relatively small staff, they operate with few managerial levels between top executives at the home office and the subsidiary. In Brazil, nearly 40 percent of the country's managers reported directly to top management in Europe, examples of what Franko terms the "mother-daughter" structure[8] (Table 2). The direct-reporting structure is most common in companies operating in relatively few countries, although several multinationals with as many as thirty foreign subsidiaries still use this structure. As we observe later, parent-subsidiary relationships in these firms retain a personal, informal atmosphere compared with many of their competitors.

The international division structure is less common among European companies. Under this structure the executive at the home office is generally responsible for all business outside Europe, but he seldom wields the power and control of his counterpart in an American company. Frequently his role is more one of coordinator, with the real authority in the hands of higher level managers.

Until recently, well-defined structural linkages between headquarters and foreign affiliates were not thought necessary by many

Table 2

Vertical Span and Structural Design of Organization by Nationality of Parent Company

| | *Vertical Span* | | | | | *Structural Design* | | | |
| | | | | | | Direct Reporting | Inter-national Division | Global Structure | Total |
Nationality	0-1	2	3-4	Total	Mean[a]				
American	17%	33%	50%	100%	2.5	0%	67%	33%	100%
European	78	18	4	100	0.9	39	17	44	100
Japanese	33	45	22	100	1.9	13	87	0	100
Total	46%	28%	26%	100%	1.8	18%	48%	34%	100%

[a]*Differences among means were compared using one-way analysis of variance. An F-test value of 19.05 was obtained, indicating differences among the means were significant at the* p < .001 *level.*

[8]Lawrence G. Franko, *European Business Strategies in the United States,* Geneve: Business International, 1971. A more recent study by Franko showed that 26 of the 70 large European MNCs still used the mother-daughter structure. Franko, 1976, *op. cit.,* p. 488.

European firms. Barriers to trade which kept national markets separate greatly reduced the need for cross-border communication. Few managers in the mother-daughter organization had supranational responsibilities. In effect, this structure became a logical outgrowth of a collection of subsidiaries held together by common ownership but not by a multinational strategy.[9] Thus, although most European firms with relatively small domestic markets became "international" early in their organizational life, their evolution to "multinational" status in a strategic sense has for many of them been a more recent phenomenon.

Reflecting this change of strategy, nearly half the European firms in the sample have adopted some form of global structure. As the parent companies changed from functional to product divisions, some firms organized their global operations around a worldwide product structure, supported by functional and area staff.[10] Far fewer organized around geographic regions, and several continue to operate with a mixed or matrix design. The distinctions between product and geographic structures, however, are less clear cut than we described earlier. As one European executive commented to us: "You're asking me to describe the structure of jelly — it hangs together but what makes it stick is a mystery."

This absence of rigid relationships is explained by cultural dispositions as well as by the history of European multinationals. In the early days of overseas investment, home office executives were not so concerned with managerial control as they were with profitable entrepreneurial ventures. Men were sent abroad and were expected to run the business independently, maintaining little more than a profit-remitting relationship with the home office.[11] In effect, managers were told to "go with God and send home the profits." The absence of direct control created little need for an elaborate organization to handle foreign operations. As a result, subsidiary managers reported to top management when necessary but generally received little guidance or support from the home office. When interaction was required, it was handled infor-

---

[9]Franko, 1976, *op. cit.,* p. 193.
[10]Franko observed that 38 of 81 large multinationals had announced a major reorganization since 1966, generally retiring their holding-company or direct-reporting structure and creating several product divisions, each with worldwide responsibility. Franko, 1975, *op. cit.,* p. 494.
[11]Stopford, *op. cit.,* p. 89.

mally, through personal visits and personnel transfers. Managers ran their own businesses and improved them by learning from their own mistakes.

The reduction of trade barriers and the diminishing importance of cartelization have changed the environmental picture for European firms. In response, many have altered their organization structure and management systems. Some European executives in our survey still prefer a direct-reporting relationship for the decision-making freedom it affords. One executive remarked to us: "This system works just fine. The superintendent (chief executive) of the mother company is much too busy to worry about me. If I see him once a year that's enough." Another manager voiced his disdain for home office staff support, noting that "I get along fine with my enemies; it's the 'helpers' (coordinators) at headquarters that give me trouble."

Regardless of the preferences expressed by today's managers, the changes occurring in European firms are likely to continue. Many of the larger and more diversified European multinationals look very much like their American counterparts,[12] and for reasons discussed in subsequent chapters, a process more fundamental than cultural or historical differences may be fostering these changes.

Japanese Organizations. In terms of overseas manufacturing, most Japanese companies are recent members of the multinational club. A brief look at their history provides a better understanding of the events leading to their current situation.

After World War II Japan's primary task was to reconstruct its industrial complex and to serve its huge domestic market. In the 1950s the Japanese turned to exports, generally through trading companies, as a means of expanding the insular market and earning much-needed foreign reserves. Ventures into foreign direct investment came slowly and cautiously. Until 1966 Japan had invested less than $200 million overseas, much of this in extractive industries. Japan's success in exporting in some ways forced its multinationals to become more involved in overseas manufacturing. By the late 1960s the country's foreign reserves became embarrassingly large, and foreign markets for exports were being

[12]Kjell-Arne Ringbakk, "Multinational Planning and Strategy." Paper presented to the Academy of International Business, San Francisco, December 1974.

closed. In recent years Japanese firms have attempted to overcome these problems through heavy investments in production capacity and market development outside Southeast Asia.

With the rapid growth of export sales, the export divisions gained considerable power in Japanese firms. In the early stages of foreign manufacturing, subsidiary managers reported to the export department, "the logic being that the *raison d'être* of the foreign manufacturing subsidiaries was to perpetuate export from Japan."[13] In many firms, however, the foreign subsidiaries soon became a burden to the export department, since it had neither the expertise nor the interest to support them properly. Furthermore, subsidiaries frequently became competitors of the export departments as host countries began to require exports by the local subsidiary.

Under pressures to modify their structures, most Japanese firms followed a pattern similar to that of U.S. multinational corporations. By the time the firms had established four manufacturing subsidiaries abroad, 80 percent of the fifty companies studied by Yoshino had created an international staff to deal specifically with foreign manufacturing affiliates.[14] Our results are similar, showing that 87 percent of the Japanese firms surveyed had developed some form of international division (Table 2).

Within this broad structure, we observed great variation in the function and design of the international division. Some had only a rudimentary staff to assist subsidiaries, often as coordinators and expediters to harmonize relations with the export department. As the number of subsidiaries grew, the staffs also expanded in size and importance within the firm. Nonetheless the struggle for independence by the international division was neither simple nor easily won, because export divisions strove to maintain their dominant stature in the firm.

Erosion of competitive advantages gradually forced the international division to strengthen its supportive role with its foreign affiliates. Regional or worldwide planning and closer controls and coordination became essential for survival. As Yoshino observes, "When the firm's international operations were confined to a small import-substitution type of investment, control did not pose much of a problem. In contrast, for new major manufacturing subsid-

---

[13]Yoshino, *op. cit.*, p. 131.
[14]*Ibid*, p. 139

iaries, the capital commitment was large and export from the parent company was substantially reduced if not totally replaced."[15]

Since exports still generate most of the foreign sales in Japanese multinationals, the export division continues to coexist with the international division. In contrast, export activities in American companies are typically assumed by the international division. Again, unlike in their American counterparts, in the Japanese companies neither the export nor the international division operates independently of domestic divisions. Another influence on structure is the Ringi system, a method of consensus decision making common to Japanese firms. This system creates a structure in which the responsibilities of the managers are less defined.

Whether Japanese firms will eventually adopt some form of global structure remains to be seen. The physical and cultural distance between Japan and its major overseas markets, in addition to its large home market, may hinder the shift to a global structure of the form described earlier. This does not imply, however, that other changes will not be forthcoming, because many Japanese subsidiary managers in our survey were extremely critical and distinctly unhappy with the present form of international organization. Changes will occur as the international group continues to evolve into an integrated, full-support division, but the precise forms of these changes remain uncertain.

North American Organizations.   Compared with European and Japanese companies, the typical American organization appears "taller," "fatter," more rigid, and in some ways more decentralized. Foreign operations in most companies are still managed by an international division responsible for exports and overseas manufacturing. Historically, the huge home-market opportunities reduced the pressure on American companies to expand abroad until they were mature and well established. Thus, when these companies entered foreign markets, they generally moved from a position of strength in their home market. Initially, foreign markets were considered small and immature compared with the domestic market.

Given these historical conditions, it is not surprising that American companies tended to treat exports and overseas affiliates as something separate from domestic operations. Because most do-

---

[15]*Ibid.*

mestic managers had limited foreign experience — and often little incentive to assist foreign affiliates — the international division became a natural center for supporting and coordinating the firm's overseas effort. The division tended to evolve early in the firm's foreign experience, normally before it acquired its fifth overseas subsidiary.[16]

In our survey all but one American company had at least five foreign subsidiaries, and not one of these parent companies used the direct-reporting system still prevalent among European countries. Two-thirds were organized around an international division, which in turn was generally divided into three or more regional offices (Table 2). The remaining companies had adopted a global structure of some form. A 1966 study of American corporations showed that 85 percent used an international division.[17] Our lower figures suggest that in the preceding decade some companies have in fact moved from an international division to other forms.

As long as a company's foreign business remains relatively small, the international division tends to serve its purpose well. The divisional vice-president acts as the spokesman and coordinator for diverse activities around the world. The division often combines substantial geographical and functional expertise in handling the idiosyncracies of foreign markets.

As overseas operations increase, however, the advantages of the international division begin to wane, because, although it is organizationally equivalent to domestic divisions, its autonomy is not equal. For product and technical expertise the international division must rely on the cooperation and assistance of the domestic divisions, a dependence that spawns stress and conflict as the calls for help become more frequent. Product-division managers, who are evaluated on domestic profits, are reluctant to devote their time and effort to overseas operations. Sometimes the domestic divisions even compete with overseas affiliates for the same business in third-country markets. Domestic managers become upset when the overseas company does not service a customer who may be important to the home division. Conversely, the attitude overseas ranges from a feeling of neglect by domestic divisions to one of exploitation over the charges it must pay to the

[16]Stopford and Wells, *op. cit.*, p. 21.
[17]National Industrial Conference Board, *The Changing Role of the International Executive,* Study in Business Policy No. 119, (New York: National Industrial Conference Board, 1966), p. 8.

domestic division for new products, technology, and other services.

During the past decade many American companies have tried to ease these conflicts by replacing the international division with a global structure. The most popular global structure charges each product or business group with worldwide responsibility. Under this system each domestic division, in effect, becomes a worldwide division responsible for profits at home and overseas. For diversified and research-oriented companies this system reduces the problems of technology transfer noted above. It also facilitates production efficiencies, sourcing decisions, customer service, and marketing strategy on a worldwide basis.

In many ways, American multinationals have come almost full circle, from a simple system relying on direct reporting, to an increasingly intricate structure revolving around an international division, and finally to a less complicated global system. In the third stage the size and complexity of foreign operations have created the need for a simpler system — one that gives overseas managers more direct access to top-level corporate executives. In this respect American companies appear to be taking a lesson from the Europeans, just as the Europeans seem to be learning other lessons, such as strategic planning and the development of more complex support structures, from their American competitors.

Company Size and Foreign Commitment

Besides the parent company's nationality, other characteristics may also mold the firm's choice of organization structure. The size of the company is frequently mentioned as an important influence, although the exact effects are far from clear.[18]

Size can be measured in many ways, including annual world sales, number of employees, units of production, or worldwide plant capacity. Since some of these measures are not comparable — for example, where products, capital intensities, and production techniques differ widely among markets — we relied on

[18]Kimberly's review of some 80 studies demonstrates the theoretical and empirical ambiguity which still surrounds the relationship between an organization's size and structure. See John R. Kimberly, "Organizational Size and the Structuralist Perspective: A Review, Critique and Proposal," *Administrative Science Quarterly,* Vol. 21, (1976), pp. 571–97.

Table 3

Influence of Size and Foreign Commitment on Vertical Span and Structural Design of Organization

| | | Foreign Sales | | |
Organization Variable	Worldwide Sales of Parent Company (millions of U.S. dollars)	Percent of Worldwide Sales	Volume (millions of U.S. dollars)	Number of Foreign Manufacturing Subsidiaries
Vertical span	.26[a]†	−.48†	.05	.27†
Structural design				
Direct reporting	$1870[b]	59.4%	$1040	10.7
International division	4796	30.9	1300	22.4
Global structure	3064	61.2	1647	25.9
ANOVA F value	1.2	16.2†	.5	4.0*

[a]*Figure represents Kendall Tau coefficient of correlation between the vertical span measure and the logarithm of the size measure.*
[b]*Figures represent means for each structural class.*
*p < .05.   †p < .01.

annual world sales. The results in Table 3 suggest that the number of levels in the hierarchy increases significantly with the level of annual sales. In terms of structural design, firms with direct-reporting structures were $1.2 billion smaller on average than those with global structures, and nearly $3 billion smaller than those with international divisions.

When a firm organizes for international operations, its commitment to foreign markets becomes a strong determinant of its structure. In effect, structure is modified to reflect changes in the corporation's strategy of foreign diversification. Our survey measured three conditions which reflect the extent of this foreign commitment:

• Proportion of worldwide sales exported from the domestic market or manufactured abroad, excluding intracompany transfers.
• Dollar volume of these sales.
• Number of countries in which the firm operates manufacturing facilities, either wholly or jointly owned.

Table 3 reports the relationship between each of the three measures and the structural variables described earlier. The number of foreign subsidiaries affects structure in a manner similar to that noted by Stopford and Wells.[19] Firms with the fewest subsidiaries tended to operate with direct-reporting structures, whereas those with the most subsidiaries used global structures. The volume of foreign sales showed a similar relationship, but the results were not significant.

Counter to commonly held expectations, the proportion of foreign sales was not related to organization structure. The explanation is probably linked to the nationality of the firm rather than its foreign commitment. As we observed in Chapter 1, European firms had higher proportions of foreign sales, and in Table 2 we noted that they also tended to choose direct-reporting or global structures.

It is noteworthy that the number of subsidiaries and the proportion of foreign sales operated independently of one another.[20] Similarly, their linkage with organization structure is disparate. As the firm becomes more dependent on foreign business (degree of dependence measured by proportion of foreign sales), the shorter chain of command reflects the tendency in many firms for headquarters to become more involved in strategic decisions and resource transfers in its foreign empire. As the number of foreign subsidiaries increases, however, so does the complexity of operations, and a longer chain of command results. Managing this complexity while at the same time avoiding long chains of communication is a critical problem in designing an organization structure. This fact helps to explain why some firms create regional or area offices. Subdivisions often retain considerable decision-making autonomy, which helps to overcome the additional link in the chain of command from headquarters to subsidiary executives.

Industry or Product Type

Textbook examples of companies using a particular structure often leave the impression that all firms in a sector choose their structures in almost sheeplike patterns. For example, oil companies rely on functional structures; pharmaceutical companies use

[19]Stopford and Wells, *op. cit.*
[20]The correlation coefficient between the two variables is $.12, p > .10$.

international divisions; and firms with diverse product lines, such as the chemical industry, use worldwide product structures. Research by Stopford and Wells established a linkage between structure and foreign product diversity, namely that greater product diversity encouraged a global structure of some form.[21] Beyond this study, however, little empirical work has been done on the relationship.

Our research included two measures dealing with technology or industry grouping. The first variable measured the relative level of capital intensity required to manufacture the principal product of the firm. Expert opinion was used to classify each firm in a low, medium, or high capital intensity category. To illustrate, food and pharmaceutical firms were classified as low in relative capital requirements; manufacturers of cars, trucks, and buses were placed in the high category. The second measure classified each firm in the survey into one of the six industries defined in Appendix D.

Statistical analysis of the relationships between the two variables and our two measures of structure — vertical span and structural design — indicated no important linkages. Tables 1 and 2 of Appendix A (at the back of the book), however, suggest that when the effects of such variables as nationality or size are removed, some industries and technologies do influence structure. Firms with greater capital intensity and those in the textile and office equipment industries operated through more levels of hierarchy. Similarly, companies in the pharmaceutical industry and those high in capital needs tended to avoid direct-reporting structure. Thus, technology and product characteristics may well influence the type of structure used abroad.

The Foreign Subsidiary

Characteristics and market conditions of a specific foreign affiliate may also shape its structural relationship to headquarters. As a practical matter an enterprise operating in many foreign markets cannot permit its formal structure to be molded by the needs of one affiliate. In cases where a small number of affiliates are particularly important to the global corporation, however, the organization structure might be expected to reflect this condition.

[21]Stopford and Wells, *op. cit.*, p. 41.

Four measures of subsidiary importance and experience were included in our survey. Two dealt with the size of the subsidiary, level of annual sales, and level of annual sales as a proportion of worldwide sales. In each case, as size increases, the hierarchical chain is compressed (see Table 1 of Appendix A). As the subsidiary reaches a certain relative size (approximately 5 percent of world sales), the hierarchy is further compressed and the structure is modified to permit closer association between the home office and the subsidiary managers. Affiliates of this importance often sense the tightening grip of headquarters as it becomes more involved in subsidiary affairs.

Two other measures considered the experience and strategic direction of the subsidiary. These variables included:

- Extent of product diversification (the number of major product lines manufactured).
- Number of years of manufacturing experience.

In each case the cross-tabular analysis indicated no relationship between structure and either strategy or experience. Thus, although product diversification by the parent company may influence structure, the relative diversification of any one subsidiary played no role in structural design. Likewise, subsidiaries with more tenure abroad than others are not necessarily more decentralized in terms of hierarchy.

To this point the analysis has primarily focused on simple two-variable analysis of the linkages between certain characteristics of the firm and its choice of structure. Readers interested in the more informative analysis of multivariate effects on structure are referred to Appendix A. For each dependent measure, the combined effects of the characteristics described above explained a high percentage of the variation in the choice of structure.

DESIGNING THE SUBSIDIARY STRUCTURE

The organizational structure of the foreign subsidiary must respond to two sets of often-conflicting pressures. First, the size, product diversity, and market conditions of the foreign affiliate encourage a structure adapted to its local environment. To the extent that local circumstances differ around the world, a firm might end up operating with a variety of structures at the subsidiary level.

A second set of forces, however, often dominates the structure decision. Whether by design or by an almost subconscious evolution, the structures of most subsidiaries in our survey reflected a mirror image, reduced in size, of the parent company. Although the mirror image facilitated communications and understanding between subsidiary and domestic managers, in some cases the subsidiary structure was not well adapted to local conditions.

The evolution of the subsidiary's structure often parallels on a smaller scale that of the parent at an earlier period. Younger subsidiaries, such as the Japanese, or those with limited sales tend to operate through a functional structure. In these firms, responsibility is divided among three or more directors — for example, finance, production, commercial — each in charge of a specific functional area. A president or managing director retains final authority over the functional managers. This design corresponds closely with the structure observed at headquarters of the European firms using a direct-reporting system.

In a divisional structure the operating divisions or product groups in the organization are elevated to a position just below the subsidiary president or managing director. In a few firms an executive vice-president might intervene, but in general the divisional directors hold the chief responsibility for all functional activities within the product group. Reporting to the president as well is a cadre of staff personnel in areas such as planning, administration, engineering, marketing, who provide counsel to all divisions. In theory this advice does not carry line authority, but we have observed numerous cases in practice where staff managers, often young, well-trained specialists, carried considerable clout and their boss's blessing when dealing with the general managers of a division.

Like the parent companies, divisional structures were most common in American subsidiaries we surveyed. In the smaller affiliates, divisional distinctions were created not along product lines, as at home, but between larger groupings, such as consumer and industrial products. The decision to divisionalize a subsidiary appeared to have been heavily influenced by the parent's structure. In no case did we observe a subsidiary organized by divisions where the parent company did not also follow a similar structure.

For firms using a global structure organized around product groups or a matrix framework, the choice of product divisions should improve the connection between the domestic division and its foreign affiliate. Although the number of cases was limited, we observed few problems in the operating relationships of these firms. Communication channels and the modes for technical and marketing assistance were generally well defined and operable.

Companies using an international division appear to experience greater difficulties with a divisional structure at the subsidiary level. Since the line authority is held by the international division, the domestic product divisions often stand to gain little by devoting time and effort to their sister divisions abroad. Various forms of incentives and advisory relationships have been developed to overcome these problems, but they are, at best, makeshift responses to an inherent limitation of the international division structure.

Among the subsidiaries still using functional structures, some we surveyed were well beyond the stage, at least in terms of size, when product divisions might be more appropriate. Since these firms were concentrated among the Europeans still using a direct-reporting structure, the subsidiary structures are unlikely to change until the parent company undergoes a major reorganization. As observed earlier, this is occurring among many European firms.[22]

GUIDELINES FOR STRUCTURAL DESIGN

Isolating the influences on structural design at one point in time permits us to infer the probable causes underlying past and future changes in the design. Although major changes in organization structure occur with relative infrequency, minor adaptations are constantly occurring. The following section identifies the future changes, major and minor, which are likely to occur, reasons for these changes, and their possible effects on performance.

Nationality

There is no doubt that in the past, historical precedent and cultural preference were important factors in determining the way in which companies organized. However, as we elaborate in later chapters, there are strong reasons to suppose that the sharp distinctions in

[22]Stopford and Wells, *ibid.*, especially Chapters 1–5.

organization structure which today characterize European, American, and Japanese firms will blur and eventually disappear. Thus, although multinationals will still have national origins, the influence of that origin on organizational structure will be overwhelmed by other characteristics of the firm and its environment.

Nonetheless, vestiges of the managerial traditions of various national groups will persist. The French will remain very French, while American top management will retain its curious aura of bureaucratic efficiency. Likewise, the many traditions of the Japanese, including consensus decision making, employment security, and paternalism, may wither but slowly in the heat of international competition. Becoming more universal, however, will be the formal organizational structures within which traditional behavior patterns operate.

In our judgment, the variables described below will dominate the future organizational design of multinational firms. Our research suggests that these variables operate in similar ways, regardless of the firm's origin. Hence, we conclude that convergence of structures independent of a firm's nationality is likely to increase over the next decade.

Overall Size of Firm

Size is generally viewed as a crucial factor determining organizational structure. However, the size of a company as a whole seems less important for multinational firms (at least in terms of their overall organization structure) than does the extent of their foreign commitments.

Nonetheless, one important finding was unequivocal: The direct-reporting organization structure is suited only for a small company, but quickly becomes an encumbrance as the company grows. Thus, as sales revenues increase, the chief executive soon finds that he can no longer coordinate the entire enterprise.

Firms with a direct-reporting structure should begin immediately to plan for a change. As figures reported below show, such structures offer few advantages and perhaps place a drag on performance. The organization structure that succeeds the direct-reporting structure has historically been an international division, at least for U.S. and Japanese firms. Among European firms the shift is often to a global structure of some form.

Extent of Foreign Commitment

More important than size in determining structural change is the firm's degree of foreign commitment. This factor can be measured in several ways, but again, sheer volume of foreign sales is less important than the firm's relative involvement in overseas business. As the proportion of foreign sales increases, pressures arise to shorten the organizational linkages between domestic and foreign operations. The desire for this change is felt by managers at home and abroad. Headquarters begins to recognize the growing importance of foreign profits to the firm's global performance and wishes to play a larger role in strategic decisions and resource allocations. Managers in foreign countries, particularly those in larger subsidiaries, become frustrated with the delays, inattention, and stepchild status accorded by headquarters and domestic divisions. The promotion of the foreign division to "separate but equal" status in the corporate family generally improves overall relations, even though it is often associated with greater centralization of strategic decisions.

The proportion of foreign sales also influences the shift from an international division to a global structure. Precise percentages were not available from the survey, but it appears that when foreign sales account for more than 25 to 35 percent of total sales, signs of severe strain began to appear in firms still retaining the international division. Calls for communications and expertise from product divisions become frequent, but responses are difficult to obtain and coordinate. Hybrid variations of the structure are sometimes used, in effect bypassing the international division. However, for reasons discussed at length by Stopford and Wells,[23] as the international division begins to account for these significant proportions of total world sales, much of its effectiveness is lost.

A second measure of foreign commitment is the number of foreign subsidiaries. In this instance the number of affiliates is closely tied to reporting relationships and communication channels. An increasing number of foreign subsidiaries soon forces a shift away from a direct-reporting structure, since growth in numbers of subsidiaries quickly surpasses the ability of the chief executive alone to meet the demands of his expanding empire.

With an international division, similar pressures for change arise when the firm moves beyond twenty to twenty-five foreign sub-

[23]*Ibid.*

sidiaries. In some firms this number of affiliates might mean that foreign sales as a proportion of world sales are approaching the breaking point described above. In others the proportion of sales may still be low, because of the presence of many small affiliates, but the complexity of coordinating so many subsidiaries becomes unmanageable. Depending on the nature of the products and markets, the international division must eventually be retired in favor of a global structure. Our survey identified several American firms with thirty or more subsidiaries which still use an international division. In several instances, however, hybrid structures had developed within the international division to deal with one product group or another. For others the hierarchy, though fossilized, was used, but managers complained bitterly about bureaucratic red tape and lack of needed support from headquarters.

In summary, it is clear that both the proportion of foreign sales and the number of foreign subsidiaries are factors which must be carefully monitored by multinational management. As each increases, there is need for modification of structure, and at certain levels these pressures become remorseless. Although many larger multinationals seem to be choosing a global structure to replace the international division, this could perhaps be only a resting point as firms seek to find an even better design. Multinationals such as Citibank, Unilever, and others, which devote extensive resources to creating an optimal structure, continue to search for the delicate balance and proper organizational "distance" between foreign affiliates and headquarters. To date, most of these changes involve minor alterations to the global structure form, often in the direction of less rigid structures and dual-reporting relationships.

Characteristics of Particular Subsidiaries

It seems plausible that particular conditions at an individual subsidiary might create the need for appropriate organizational relationships. In our study, increases in both the absolute and the relative size of the subsidiary led to shorter chains of command. Thus, increased size of the subsidiary fostered greater interest and involvement by headquarters, concern that generally led to a tightening of reins over the subsidiary, at least for major strategic decisions. Managers of larger subsidiaries may well view their newfound stardom with mixed emotions — enjoying the limelight and attention on the one hand, but abhorring the closer overview by the home office on the other.

Does the Right Structure Pay Off?

The ultimate question in designing a structure is whether it will lead to improved performance. Any analysis seeking to link structure to performance is difficult, first because performance results from an amalgam of many conditions. Financial performance can be associated with sectoral conditions, market positions for the firm's major products, trade-offs between future growth and profits today, and many other factors. Secondly, there is virtually no way to be certain that changes in profits were influenced directly by the choice of structure.

With these caveats in mind, we examined the relationship between organization structure and the performance firms in our Brazilian sample. Performance in this case was measured by the profitability of the Brazilian subsidiaries.

Table 4 shows that the subsidiary profitability of firms using a direct-reporting structure ranked well below that of firms using other structures. In his study of European multinationals operating in the United States, Franko reached similar conclusions: In this

Table 4

Profitability of Subsidiary by Structural Design of Organization

Organization Variable	Profitability Measure			
	Return on Equity	Return on Assets	Operating Return on Assets	Return on Sales
Structural design				
Direct reporting	10.5%[a]	4.9%	26.2%	4.1%
International division	16.8	9.1	29.0	8.0
Global structure	25.3	10.2	31.5	7.4
Total	19.1%	8.7%	29.4%	7.0%
Vertical span	.03[b]	.07	.12	.15

[a]*Figures reported as means of pretax profitability.*
[b]*Figure represents a Kendall Tau coefficient of correlation of vertical span with the profitability measure.*

case subsidiaries with a "mother-daughter" (that is, direct-reporting) structure experienced much slower growth than those with other structures.[24]

During the early days of a subsidiary's operation there may well be advantages to direct reporting. With heavy infusions of capital and management expertise, close linkages with the chief executive can be beneficial, if he and his staff have adequate time to assist the fledgling affiliate. For reasons elaborated earlier, however, these benefits quickly disappear as the subsidiary matures or as more foreign affiliates are established.

Differences in the performance of firms with structures other than direct reporting showed that those with global structures reported a slight edge over those with international divisions, but the differences were small. Since some of the firms with international divisions were clearly in need of reorganization, these results might be viewed as lending some credence to the findings of Stopford and Wells[25] showing that firms with severe mismatches between strategy and structure performed well below those with appropriate matches.

In conclusion, the results, though tentative, tend to support the theoretical premise that structure should be appropriate for the strategy being pursued and that changes in strategic directions require appropriate structural responses. Our analysis suggests that the term strategy must be defined broadly, to include measurement of the firm's foreign commitment, whether by proportion of sales or number of foreign subsidiaries.

SUMMARY

The organizational structure of the multinational firm provides the framework within which the home office attempts to coordinate, communicate with, and control its foreign operations. Each company is unique in some respects in the way it handles these functions; consequently, its organizational structure must be shaped and molded to meet its specific needs. Despite the idiosyncracies of individual companies and national origins, nationality of the parent company is likely to play a declining role in the choice of organization structure.

[24]Franko, 1971, *op. cit.*
[25]Stopford and Wells, *op. cit.*, p. 80.

Most American companies, long accustomed to operating from a large home-market base, still distinguish rather sharply between home and overseas business. To handle their foreign business, many of them remain committed to the international division. Substantial increases in the absolute and relative importance of overseas sales and manufacturing have stimulated a plethora of cosmetic changes to relieve the inevitable strains on such a structure. In many companies, however, these modifications have not sufficed, and recently a number of large American companies have adopted a global approach similar to that found in some of the European firms.

Long accustomed to doing business outside their home markets, European structures typically do not distinguish sharply between foreign and domestic business. Relative to most American firms, the Europeans tend to centralize more authority in the hands of a few top executives. Consequently their organizational hierarchy shows fewer levels between top executives at the home office and overseas. The evidence suggests that the pattern of personal, informal control is shifting in the direction of more formal standardized procedures.

As relative newcomers to foreign manufacturing, the Japanese multinationals find themselves in a state of organizational evolution. The international division has replaced the export department in virtually all companies with substantial foreign business, but the size and services provided by the division vary widely from firm to firm.

Despite the fact that current organization structures show more than mere vestigial traces of historical precedence and cultural preference, we are convinced that such factors will play a diminishing role in explaining differences of organization structure. In most organizations important issues and problems relating to structure tend to arise without regard to cultural distinctions, and in this sense the trend seems universal. In the past these problems were often resolved in ways which led to distinctive structural designs consistent with fundamental cultural tenets. For the multinational organization today, the increasing comparability of environmental and strategic conditions, embracing almost all the world's major markets and a common set of multinational competitors, encourages the adoption of a more geocentric perspective.

Chapter **3**

Planning in the Multinational Enterprise

Coordinating the activities of diverse operations around the globe greatly complicates the planning process for the multinational firm. Whereas most larger companies have adopted formalized systems for standardizing the planning formats received at headquarters, the degree of integration of subsidiary strategies varies widely from firm to firm.

Headquarters plays a central role in developing both the planning process and the esprit de corps so important to effective planning. These home office functions have been examined by numerous investigators, and so are not dealt with here in detail.[1] Similarly, the interesting issues of standardized strategies and programs are considered in Chapter 4.[2]

[1]Kjell-Arne Ringbakk, "Multinational Planning and Strategy." Paper presented to the Academy of International Business, San Francisco, December 1974; Kjell-Arne Ringbakk, "Strategic Planning in a Turbulent International Environment," *Long-Range Planning,* June 1976, pp. 2–11; Peter Lorange, "A Framework for Strategic Planning in Multinational Corporations," *Long-Range Planning,* June 1976, pp. 30–37; Derek F. Channon, "Prediction and Practice in Multinational Strategic Planning," *Long-Range Planning,* April 1976, pp. 50–57; George A. Steiner and Hans Schöllhammer, "Pitfalls in Multinational Long-Range Planning," *Long-Range Planning,* April 1975, pp. 2–11; Warren J. Keegan, "A Conceptual Framework for Multinational Marketing," *Columbia Journal of World Business,* November–December 1972, pp. 67–76.
[2]R. J. Aylmer, "Who Makes Marketing Decisions in the Multinational Firms?" *Journal of Marketing,* Vol. 34 (October 1970), pp. 25–30; Robert Buzzell, "Can You Standardize Multinational Marketing?" *Harvard Business Review,* Vol. 46,

This chapter concentrates on plans and planning at the subsidiary level — what activities are planned, who becomes involved, how it gets done, the pitfalls encountered, and suggestions for improving the process. Whether plans are being prepared for domestic or foreign purposes, the process must begin with a market analysis, a task for which the subsidiary should bear primary responsibility. Beyond this, the foreign subsidiary must plan to satisfy the needs of its local market, as well as the requests of headquarters to manufacture products for various foreign markets. Pressures from both sides, the local market and headquarters, force trade-offs and problems in the planning process, issues discussed below.

ISSUES IN SUBSIDIARY PLANNING

The turbulent environments of the 1970s have drawn renewed attention to planning problems;[3] and perhaps because of the greater uncertainty, more multinationals have begun to plan their overseas activities with the same degree of care received by domestic operations.[4] The emphasis on better planning was also stimulated by the movement toward greater interdependence among the far-flung operations. How these shifts occurred and the

No. 6, (November–December 1968), pp. 102–113; S. Watson Dunn (ed.), *International Handbook of Advertising* (New York: McGraw-Hill, 1964); "The Case Study Approach in Cross-Cultural Research," *Journal of Marketing Research,* Vol. 3, No. 1 (February 1966), pp. 26–31; "Effect of National Identity on Multinational Promotion Strategy in Europe," *Journal of Marketing,* Vol. 40, No. 4 (October 1976), pp. 50–57; Erik Elender, "International Advertisers Must Devise Universal Ads," *Advertising Age,* November 27, 1961, pp. 91–96; Arthur C. Fatt, "The Danger of 'Local' Advertising," *Journal of Marketing,* Vol. 31, No. 1 (January 1967), pp. 61–62; Warren J. Keegan, "Multinational Product Planning: Strategic Alternatives," *Journal of Marketing,* Vol. 33, No. 1 (January 1969), pp. 58–62; John K. Ryans, Jr., and James H. Donnelley, Jr., "Standardized Global Advertising, A Call As Yet Unanswered," *Journal of Marketing,* Vol. 33, No. 3 (April 1969), pp. 57–60; Ralph Z. Sorenson and Ulrich E. Wiechmann, "How Multinationals View Marketing Standardization," *Harvard Business Review,* Vol. 53 (May–June 1975), pp. 38–167; Ulrich E. Wiechmann, "Integrating Multinational Marketing Activities," *Columbia Journal of World Business,* Vol. 9, No. 4 (Winter 1974), pp. 7–16; Yoran Wind, Susan Douglas, and Howard Perlmutter, "Guidelines for Developing International Marketing Strategies," *Journal of Marketing,* Vol. 37, No. 2 (April 1973), pp. 14–23.

[3]"Corporate Planning: Piercing Future Fog in the Executive Suite," *Business Week,* April 28, 1975, pp. 46–50.

[4]Ringbakk, 1976, *op. cit.*

quality of planning that resulted, however, differ widely from firm to firm, particularly between nationality groups.

Regardless of the planning evolution which has occurred in their companies, managers generally concur with the judgment that their current planning practices leave a great deal to be desired.[5] The most common criticisms are that much of the planning effort is operational, not strategic, in orientation; that too much reliance is placed on financially oriented control systems; that bottom-up and top-down components of the planning process are poorly integrated; and that there are too many instances of misunderstanding or actual deceit in the planning relationships between headquarters and foreign subsidiaries. Thus, although the need for more effective planning has increased, improvements in the practice of planning have not kept pace.

Some of the key planning problems revolve around the home office/subsidiary relationship, and cover such issues as:

- Where and by whom different types of plans should be developed, home office or subsidiary.
- The extent to which headquarters should specify and direct the planning process.
- How to balance the headquarter's need for control and the subsidiary's desire for flexibility, and still achieve the purposes of the planning process.

Although these problems are not dissimilar from those encountered by domestic divisions, several factors — not the least of which is geographic distance — exacerbate the stresses. In the past these difficulties were effectively eliminated by not planning. Subsidiary managers received near-absolute authority to run the foreign affiliate; in European firms, for example, headquarters often played a very passive role. Foreign subsidiaries were viewed as a portfolio of diverse investments, and whatever planning was done at the subsidiary was tailored to the requirements of the local market.

This practice has changed dramatically since the mid-sixties. In many firms resources are no longer allocated to subsidiaries on the basis of past performance, or even current needs, but in a way designed to optimize returns of the total corporation. Thus pro-

---

[5]See, for example, Sidney M. Robbins and Robert B. Stobaugh, ''The Best Measuring Stick for Foreign Subsidiaries,'' *Harvard Business Review,* September – October 1973, pp. 80 – 88, or Channon, *op. cit.,* Lorange, *op. cit.*

duction, marketing, and financial decisions are being made with an increasing emphasis on the global needs of the corporation. Plans that incorporate and explicate such decisions must necessarily be coordinated and approved by some central management group.

This flexing of the headquarter's muscle in the planning process has occurred simultaneously with other important trends, some of which have increased the pressures for decentralized planning and increased autonomy for subsidiaries. These trends include such factors as:

- Host-country efforts to make foreign firms more responsive to local needs.
- Increased economic and political turbulence.
- Keener competition by both local and foreign firms in overseas markets.
- Increasing customer sophistication, particularly in rapidly growing Third World markets.

The conflicts which result from the opposing forces between headquarters and foreign subsidiary frequently lead to considerable wasted effort and ineffectiveness in the planning process. In the following discussion we attempt to show how a beneficial symbiosis can be achieved.

PLANNING SYSTEMS

While thoughtful executives for many years have carried out in some form both long- as well as short-range planning, the time periods considered and the comprehensiveness of the effort varied greatly,with the situation and the outlook of the executive.[6]

The Role of Planning

Warren's appraisal of planning practices in the United States in the mid-sixties seems equally valid for most multinational subsidiaries today. There is, however, an almost frenetic effort underway to modify planning systems, as executives struggle to adapt to a more complex and hostile environment.[7] Besides increasing concern for

---

[6]E. Kirby Warren. *Long-Range Planning: The Executive Viewpoint* (Englewood Cliffs, N.J.: Prentice-Hall, 1966), p. 16.
[7]"Corporate Planning: Piercing Future Fog in the Executive Suite," *Business Week*, April 28, 1975, pp. 46–50.

greater flexibility and speed of preparation,[8] the attention of management is shifting away from the *process* of planning in favor of greater emphasis on the *content* of plans.

The subsidiary's planning system is almost invariably modeled on that of its parent. Although the subsidiary systems are generally simplified, befitting the subsidiary's small size and more limited resources, in some cases its system is as complex as the parent's domestic planning process. There are obvious advantages in coordination when similar planning systems are used, although the arguments for more simplicity at the subsidiary level are also strong.

A great many variations were observed in the depth and sophistication of planning activities as well as in the types of plans produced. In some companies the annual plan consisted of a few pages filled with elementary budget data; in others the plan consisted of several volumes, often repetitive and cumbersome. As one might expect, in many subsidiaries the plan is placed in "cold storage" soon after it is approved, and gathers dust until the next "planning season," when it is dusted off and updated for the following year. In other subsidiaries, however, the plan is very much a living document which is referred to, used, and in some cases revered. Although these differences can be partly attributed to managerial attitudes and the corporate ethos toward planning, the discussion below shows that other factors also contribute to the variations.

Planning necessitates an organized process for making decisions in the present about what the organization will do in the future. Plans, together with other elements such as standard operating procedures and habitually acquired role behaviors on the part of individuals, are key factors in the predictability of the future behavior of the organization. Plans provide action guidelines which, if followed, enable different organizational subunits to combine their individual actions in a way that helps the organization to achieve its objectives. For example, plans should provide the guidelines for ensuring that the marketing, production, and financial functions are all pulling in the same direction instead of each pulling in its own direction. It is in this manner that plans are said to act as coordinating or integrating mechanisms.

[8]*Ibid.*

It follows, therefore, that a plan developed but not followed defeats the purpose of the planning process.[9] Similarly, a plan that does not accurately reflect the status and expected direction of the enterprise is equally dangerous. Yet these problems, common to most planning systems, become particularly threatening in a multinational firm where the task of coordination is crucial but more difficult. Consider, for example, the following situation:

If the South African assembly operation and its recently added manufacturing facilities are to function smoothly and efficiently, they must today receive a carefully controlled and coordinated flow of vehicle parts and components from West Germany, England, Canada, the United States, and even Australia. These must reach General Motors of South Africa in the right time to allow an orderly scheduling of assembly without accumulation of excessive inventory.[10]

Clearly, the larger and more complex the firm, and the more its commitment to global strategies, the more pressing the need for coordination and therefore planning.

Types of Plans Prepared

In the survey it was found that the annual operating plan served as the keystone for virtually all multinational firms, except for several Japanese companies which relied on a six-month planning cycle. In most subsidiaries the operating plan became the starting point for longer range planning. American and European subsidiaries generally favored annual and five-year planning periods, a preference observed also by Ringbakk,[11] who found striking similarity between larger U.S. and European firms. Differences in planning systems between industry groups were slight, except for those requiring heavy capital investments or long retooling periods, many of which followed a seven- or ten-year long-range planning horizon.

Most subsidiaries combined their short- and long-term plans with a rolling or forward-planning system. Under the annual-plus-five-year system, for example, the second-year estimates of the old five-year plan are revised and incorporated into the new one-

[9]Note that for the time being we are assuming a stationary environment, that is, no changes have occurred which might vitiate the assumptions.
[10]Bernard M. Gross, *The Managing of Organizations* (New York: The Free Press, 1964), p. 264.
[11]Ringbakk, 1976, *op. cit.*

year plan. Projections in the long-range plan are then reviewed and modified, and a new fifth-year estimate is developed.

The popularity of the rolling system belies its inherent weaknesses, namely the frequent lack of rigor in creating the longer range plans. Years two through five may become little more than extensions of the current budget, with far too little emphasis on the assumptions and plans that should support the numbers. In the words of one manager, "After year one it's simply an exercise in fog sculpting."

To overcome this limitation several firms separated their operating and long-range planning efforts, some even following a zero-based system requiring a totally new long-range plan each year. In some instances, however, there was little liaison between those managers responsible for the long-range plan and those responsible for the annual plan, the latter sometimes emanating from the controller's office.

Similarities in the types of plans prepared obscure major differences in the breadth and depth of the formal planning effort. Unfortunately, what passed for an operating plan in many firms was little more than a detailed budget. Such companies often suffer from strategic myopia. Their preoccupation with planning as a financially oriented control device often leads to excessive rigidity, thereby limiting their abilities to respond to and initiate changes. In terms of nationality differences, American subsidiaries had the most comprehensive formal planning systems, with detailed supporting plans covering such activities as research and development (R&D), new product launches, and capital expenditures.

PREPARING THE SUBSIDIARY PLAN

The Planning Process

Figure 1 presents a crude depiction of the modal planning procedure used by the foreign subsidiaries in our survey. Several points merit attention. The first is the key role of home office in the early stages of planning. Strong evidence of central direction and control existed in one-fourth of the subsidiaries; in these cases headquarters provided a set of goals or targets that its subsidiary was expected to achieve. In other subsidiaries the home office role was limited to providing specific informational inputs — for example, global, regional, or even local economic forecasts to the planning

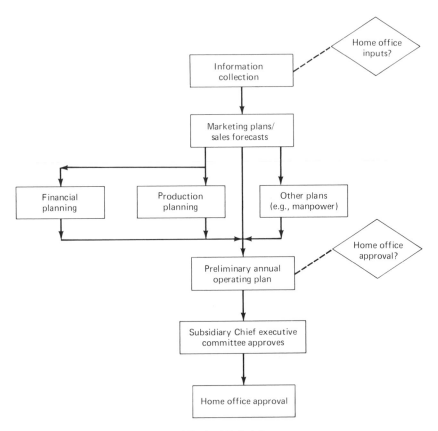

FIGURE 1   Planning Process of Typical Subsidiary

process. In yet others, headquarters played no role whatsoever at this early stage.

After the information collection phase, marketing plans and sales forecasts are developed. As in domestic U.S. planning, these provide the key volume inputs for other functional planning activities — finance, production, and manpower, for example. In multidivision subsidiaries, functional plans are developed at the divisional level, so integration into the overall operating plan is by division rather than by functional area.

Headquarters Review

In some companies the planning process is now virtually complete: the plan receives a final revision, it is put in presentation format, and it awaits only home office approval. In many firms the preliminary plan itself is forwarded to the home office for comments, revisions, and preliminary approval. In some companies several home office reviews are required before the plan is finalized.

At this stage the pace of planning activity becomes most frenetic, because most firms rely on in-person presentations and reviews. In a company without a regional headquarters, such reviews are conducted in a meeting between the subsidiary chief executive and his superior either at the home office or at the subsidiary. With regional offices, the traffic patterns become even more frequent and complex.

Nonetheless, in some subsidiaries, particularly European firms, managers do no more than prepare the plans, submit them to headquarters, and hope that the plan will be accepted without comment. As one subsidiary chief executive once remarked, "I presume they (home office) look at the plan, but we hear nothing from them." In practice, sending the final plan to the home office for "information only" is certainly the extreme situation and one leading to problems of communication and control, which are discussed in subsequent chapters.

With these few exceptions the vast majority of subsidiaries always need formal home office approval before the plan can be adopted. In American companies it is common for the subsidiary chief executive, sometimes accompanied by his management team, to present and defend the subsidiary plan personally before corporate executives. In some firms these reviews assume an aura of religious ritual. As a result, immense effort is often devoted to preparation for the presentation. In contrast, in most European companies the review process and ritual is generally less elaborate. As we observe below, a comprehensive review process, such as the practice of sending goals down from headquarters, reflects the company's overall control strategy and the degree of integration in the planning process.

Developing the Sales Forecast

The effectiveness of a plan and the accuracy of a forecast are dependent on the quality of associated informational inputs. Both top-down and bottom-up sources play a part in subsidiary marketing planning. Top-down inputs come from higher levels in the organization, often home office staff, and include aggregate economic and market projections, planning guides, and information from a marketing research department. Bottom-up inputs derive from lower levels in the organization, including such sources as salesmen, distributors, and other intermediary or final customers. In this case the information flows upward to the marketing manager or someone else responsible for collecting and interpreting data.[12]

Over 60 percent of the firms in our sample used some form of bottom-up forecasting. Salesmen and dealer forecasts were key inputs; the Japanese relied on this information more heavily than subsidiaries of other nationalities, perhaps because their planning infrastructure was less fully developed. Obtaining good data is one of the major problems of subsidiary marketing planning, and under such conditions bottom-up approaches are particularly useful. They offer a means for gathering the best available information from important components of the company's distribution system. Moreover, this information not only supports the development of gross sales forecasts, but also enables a product-by-product and market-by-market analysis as well as the establishment of competitive sales levels and market potential.[13] These data are crucial to effective planning, and may not be otherwise accessible to subsidiary planners. Bottom-up forecasting also encourages widespread participation in the planning process, and since many executives noted that increased participation was an explicit planning goal, many firms had taken steps toward this end by using some form of bottom-up forecasting.

Creating Forecasts, Budgets, and Quotas

The concepts of forecasts, budgets, and quotas are frequently confused and misused. The sales forecast refers to the level of sales the company expects to attain in a given period under a particular marketing plan.[14] In addition to the sales forecast, two other quan-

[12]John U. Farley and James M. Hulbert, "Sistemas de Planejamento Mercadologico de Una Firma Multinacional Sediada no Brazil," *Revista de Administracāo de Empresas,* Vol. 15, No. 1 (January–February 1975), pp. 7–14.

[13]James M. Hulbert, "Composite Forecasting Systems: Avoiding the Pitfalls and Problems." Working Paper, Columbia University, April 1978; Noël Capon and James M. Hulbert, "Decision Systems Analysis in Industrial Marketing," *Industrial Marketing Management,* Vol. 4 (1975), pp. 143–160.

[14]Thomas R. Wotruba, *Sales Management: Planning, Accomplishment, and Evaluation* (New York: Holt, Rinehart and Winston, 1970), p. 54.

titative estimates must usually be developed: sales quota and sales budget. The sales quota acts as a target or goal to stimulate selling effort. Because the purpose of sales quotas is to motivate, managers often set such quotas higher than the "best estimate" forecast. On the other hand, the sales budget provides the estimated revenues used for such purposes as planning cash flows. Unlike the sales quota, the sales budget is frequently estimated on the conservative side, apparently because being over budget is more acceptable than being under budget. This practice is common — and indeed is often suggested in management literature[15] — provided the different sets of figures are not confused or misused.

The figures in Table 1 indicate that for Brazilian subsidiaries the practice of raising the forecasts to set sales quotas was far more common in American companies. Similarly, the Americans were more inclined to lower their forecasts for budgeting purposes. In our judgment the prevalence of this practice in American companies results in large part from the strong pressures placed on the managers of these subsidiaries to meet their planning commitments. "Puffed up" sales quotas put more pressure on the sales force to make the short-term sale, and the conservative sales

Table 1

Raising or Lowering Sales Forecasts for Quotas or Budgeting, by Nationality of Company

Nationality of Parent Company	Set Sales Quotas above Forecasts[a]						Lower Forecasts for Sales Budget[a]					
	Do		Do Not		Total		Do		Do Not		Total	
	%	No.	%	No.	Number		%	No.	%	No.	Number	
American	42%	11	58%	15	26		45%	13	55%	16	29	
European	24	6	76	19	25		28	7	72	18	25	
Japanese	20	1	80	4	5		17	1	83	5	6	
Overall totals	32%	18	68%	38	56		35%	21	65%	39	60	

[a]No significant differences by nationality in either practice when tested alone, but American companies were significantly more inclined to engage in both forecast raising and lowering than were others. (Value of chi-square = 3.98, with one degree of freedom, significant at the $p < .05$ level.)

[15]Philip Kotler, *Marketing Management: Analysis, Planning and Control* (Englewood Cliffs, N.J.: Prentice Hall, 2nd ed., (1972), p. 203.

budgets enable higher level managers to camouflage uncertain forecasting or inadequate performance. Elementary psychology provides enough insight to understand why managers resort to these practices, but problems are inherent in a system that produces such practices, problems discussed later in the chapter.

Comprehensiveness of Planning

Many companies in our survey did not seem to grasp the distinction between a budget and a plan. Perhaps the precision often associated with numbers creates a sense of confidence for the planner that is not felt when prose is used. As a result, the annual plan often becomes an exercise in generating numbers for the following activities:

- Forecasting sales.
- Estimating production levels and costs, manpower and supply needs, and sometimes future capacity needs.
- Developing projections of capital expenditures and cash flows.

The resulting "plan" is a two- to fifteen-page document filled with numbers and little else. Although such data are useful and necessary for developing plans, the document described may represent a budget, not a plan.

A comparison of these documents with the 300–500 page volumes prepared by some subsidiaries illustrates the marked contrast in the concept of planning. These plans include the typical budgetary data as well as other key components such as:

- A review of past activities leading to the present situation.
- A thorough analysis of the economic, competitive, and customer environments.
- A clear statement of subsidiary objectives and specific directions for marketing, finance, and production.
- Product-line plans with "hard" (quantitative) objectives and specific statements of strategies and programs.
- Supporting plans for production, purchasing, finance, manpower, and other areas.

While length per se is of dubious merit in a plan, the distinction between planning and budgeting is an important one. A reliable budget can result only from a sound plan, and in the absence of such a plan, it can be argued that the budget is meaningless.

Organizational Support for Planning

In subsidiaries that have accepted the concept of planning, the process is not an annual rite but a continuous one. Finding an appropriate organizational structure for the process is therefore important, because although task forces may effectively handle the annual planning "binge," more permanent structures soon become needed.

In the European and Japanese subsidiaries the problem was often handled in a rather straightforward manner — the chief executive directly supervised the planning activities. In the European instance this practice reflected a more centralized management style; for the Japanese it seemed to occur because of the subsidiary's relatively small size in Brazil.

In American subsidiaries a committee approach was a common modus operandi. Indeed, the entire planning process tended to be much more participative. The executives of American subsidiaries generally expressed concern over trying to push the planning activity further "down" in the organization, thereby increasing the participation of lower level managers. Thus, in many American subsidiaries, the chief executive's role was important but not necessarily direct. He served as coordinator and arbitrator of disagreements, but often through his membership on a planning committee rather than through direct intervention.

Consistent with this more participative approach, American subsidiaries typically involved more line managers in the planning activity. Thus, although an increasing number of subsidiaries have their own planning departments, these groups seldom have complete planning responsibility — their role is to support line managers in their own planning. In Japanese and European subsidiaries, however, the planning department or finance function frequently carries full responsibility for planning.[16]

---

[16]There is a variety of evidence suggesting that heavy involvement of line personnel is essential for effective use of planning, though much (but not all) of this evidence is based on American experience. See, for example, John W. Brion, *Corporate Marketing Planning* (New York: John Wiley, 1967); Kjell-Arne Ringbakk, "Why Planning Fails," *European Business,* Spring 1971, pp. 15–27; "Corporate Planning: Piercing Future Fog in the Executive Suite," *Business Week,* April 28, 1975, p. 50.

HEADQUARTERS INVOLVEMENT IN SUBSIDIARY PLANNING

Function of Planning

The direction and influence of headquarters on subsidiary planning can be assessed at several levels. First, views on the purpose of and attitudes toward planning differ widely — the views of managers in American subsidiaries frequently diverging from those of managers of European and Japanese subsidiaries. When subsidiary managers were asked what they perceived as being the major benefit of the plan itself, nearly 50 percent of the Americans reported that the plan represented a commitment or target which must be achieved, whereas only 21 and 33 percent of managers in European and Japanese firms, respectively, gave this response.

For American subsidiaries the commitment typically referred to a profit target, sometimes a sales forecast, and occasionally the entire plan. Once the subsidiary chief executive "signed off" the plan, it became, in the words of one manager, "my bible; I hit it or else." Within recent years, headquarters of many American companies further increased the pressure on their subsidiaries to achieve planned targets. This sometimes led to self-protective behavior by subsidiary managers, which subverted the intentions of headquarters, problems discussed later. In contrast, within many European and Japanese subsidiaries the plan served more as a budgeting and coordinating device both for the subsidiary and for headquarters.

Formalization of Planning

A second form of headquarters involvement relates to the standardization and formalization of planning. This can occur along two dimensions, one controlling the *process* of planning and the accompanying forms and procedures, and one focusing on the *content* of plans, on seeking greater comparability, and on standardization of operating programs.

Headquarters of American and Japanese firms played the most directive role in process formalization with specifications for types of information to collect, sequencing of activities, timing, and nature of the approval process. For the annual plan, over 90 percent of American and Japanese firms in the survey followed a standard format specifying the final layout and appearance of the plans. This compares with 73 percent for European subsidiaries.

Considering that the annual plan represents a near-contractual relationship between subsidiary and headquarters for American companies, it is not surprising that these companies used a formalized process. Large European firms tended to follow a similar pattern, but the planning processes of smaller subsidiaries were typically less formalized, regardless of national origin. Perhaps size explains the relative lack of planning sophistication among Japanese subsidiaries surveyed in Brazil. Although their parent companies had followed a rather formalized process for some time,[17] the system we observed for Japanese firms was often little more than the preparation of operating budgets.

The most important implication of this finding, however, is the overwhelming dominance of standardized planning systems among subsidiaries of all three groupings. Consistent with our discussion on the expanding role of the home office, the information-processing, planning, and control activities of multinational headquarters are all facilitated by such common formats. On the other hand, the use of identical systems can also lead to the imposition of heavy demands for data, excessive desk work, and a reduction of subsidiary initiative and flexibility.

Standardized strategies and programs, which tell subsidiaries what to do instead of how to do it, might seem more controversial than a standardized process. The prevalence of truly standardized approaches, however, appears to be lower than suggested by some previous work.[18] Indeed, the amount of support and guidance from headquarters seemed to be related more to the particular strategic objectives being pursued by the subsidiary than to other factors.[19] For most firms the direct influences of headquarters were relatively selective, on a case-by-case basis. Notable exceptions were such obvious areas as branding, trademarks, and sometimes packaging. This topic is treated in more detail in Chapter 4, where we discuss the development of subsidiary strategies and programs.

[17]Ringbakk, 1974, *op. cit.*
[18]See, for example, Aylmer, *op. cit.*
[19]William K. Brandt and James M. Hulbert, "Headquarters Guidance in Marketing Strategy in the Multinational Subsidiary," *Columbia Journal of World Business,* Vol. 12, No. 4, (Winter 1977), pp. 7–14

PROBLEMS IN SUBSIDIARY PLANNING

Planning problems in a multinational firm are complicated by geographic, economic, and cultural differences between headquarters and the foreign subsidiary. Figure 2 separates some of the major problems into those originating from management behavior and those arising from the planning process. The second dimension shows whether the locus of the problem is headquarters or the foreign subsidiary. The problems identified by no means represent an exhaustive list, but they do cover the difficulties most frequently encountered in our survey. Note also that a particular problem may be symptomatic of a broader problem whose locus may lie elsewhere.

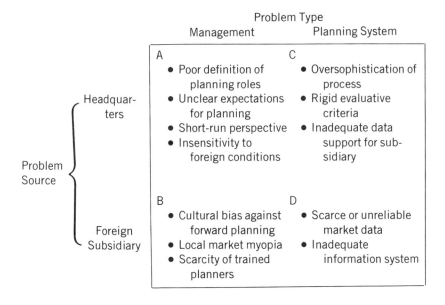

FIGURE 2   A Paradigm of Planning Problems

Headquarters Management Problems

Poor Definition of Planning Roles.   The annual operating plan is seldom a product of the subsidiary's effort alone. Headquarters often provides a variety of inputs, ranging from basic economic and market information to a few extreme cases where objectives and programs are mandated. Given the complexity of planning in a multinational enterprise, involving multiple levels of participation as well as numerous products and countries, some tensions and in'efficiencies between headquarters and subsidiary are bound to occur. Many of these difficulties could be avoided or ameliorated by better definition of the roles and responsibilities for each set of managers. Better specification of issues such as who is responsible for particular steps in the planning process, who should provide which types of data, or who should resolve conflicts would help to improve the working of the planning process. This suggestion may seem obvious, but the absence of such specification gave rise to numerous problems in the firms surveyed.

Clear definition of responsibilities generally encourages greater formalization of the planning process. Although, as noted earlier, formalization creates some problems of its own, this evolution seems inevitable as firms become more global and integrated in their planning activities. For many firms, however, formalizing the process has led to greater rigidity and centralization of the planning function. In some instances this situation occurred without clarifying the roles that subsidiary managers were to play in the process. Planning should be a force which promotes coordination and delegation of activities, yet these objectives are frequently unmet where roles are poorly understood.

Unclear Expectations.   Accompanying the failure to specify the roles of various managers in the planning process is the frequent lapse by headquarters in communicating the purpose and expectations of the planning effort. Subsidiary management is directed to implement a particular system without understanding the benefits to themselves or to anyone else. As a result they perceive the system as yet another attempt by the home office to keep a closer watch on their activities. They complete planning forms dutifully but without deriving significant benefits from the process, the reviews, or the resulting plan. Headquarters often exacerbates the problem by emphasizing the planning steps instead of the quality of planned objectives and strategies.

Short-Run Perspective.   The unrelenting drive at headquarters for increased sales and profits often creates a mentality that emphasizes short-run results over long-term growth. For American firms, in particular, this perspective, combined with the view that plans represent a performance contract between headquarters and subsidiary, results in a plan which serves as a control mechanism. The contrasting view of many European and Japanese firms, which stress planning as a means of coordinating and integrating foreign and domestic operations, embraces a desire to meet objectives, but does not emphasize achievement of short-term goals as rigidly as American companies.

Overemphasizing short-term goals can mean that the plan becomes an end in itself instead of a means to achieving objectives. Consequently, the effort is sometimes directed into internal manipulations and infighting to assure that cost and revenue projections are met. As a result data are sometimes distorted and disguised, thus leaving both headquarters and the subsidiary without a clear picture of actual results. In developing markets such as Brazil, where the long-run potential remains bright and the trade-off between growth and immediate profits might favor the former, managers complained bitterly about the short-term demands imposed by headquarters. This criticism was most often heard in American firms, where in several cases we observed weak market positions that had been strong in the past but had been inadvertently "harvested" in order to meet headquarters demand for "profits now."

Insensitivity to Foreign Conditions.   Although some tension is endemic in virtually all headquarters-subsidiary relationships, criticisms about headquarters insensitivity recurred too often to be dismissed. Part of the problem is caused by inexperience at the home office, for example the tendency to place MBA recruits in planning positions. The problem is sometimes aggravated by the home office staff being overloaded with information, often as a result of its own requests for data. Such overloading reduces responsiveness and apparent sensitivity to the often equally frenetic conditions of subsidiary managers. Finally, ethnocentric biases invariably creep into the decision process, particularly for headquarters personnel who are unfamiliar with foreign operations. In concert, these conditions create frustration and often lead to a doctoring of the data, a practice carried out at the subsidiary but fostered by the attitudes of the home office.

Subsidiary Management Problems

In discussions with subsidiary managers, headquarters is the universal scapegoat for planning problems; however, the subsidiary managers must share some of the blame for shortcomings in the planning process.

Cultural Bias against Forward Planning. In some countries cultural biases run counter to the basic concept of planning, particularly long-range planning. The problem can exist at headquarters as well as at the subsidiary; it is probably more common in subsidiaries operating in Third World markets, where a "live for today" attitude is more prevalent.

Local Market Myopia. An element of gamesmanship sometimes arises when subsidiary management dedicates itself to furthering the growth and profit of the subsidiary even at the expense of the broader interests of the worldwide company. Even when such behavior is not deliberate, resistance to home office directives may still arise. Excessive home office emphasis on short-term sales and profits can encourage this conflict, especially when subsidiary management is more concerned about long-term market development.

Whether the origins of such problems lie with headquarters or with the subsidiary, ineffective planning is often the result. Planning data may be collected, the forms completed, and the plans submitted for review, but merely going through the motions does not constitute effective planning. Without a joint commitment, the exercise is of very limited value.

Scarcity of Trained Planners. Planning problems are worsened by the chronic shortages of well-trained managers (and planners) in less developed countries. Too few home office executives seem to comprehend fully the limited manpower resources with which subsidiaries are managed.

Headquarters Planning System Problems

Oversophistication of Planning Process. The chief criticisms made by subsidiary managers about the planning process center on its complexity and inflexibility. Both processes and materials imposed on foreign subsidiaries are commonly derived from the systems used by domestic divisions. These are often too sophisticated, detailed, and cumbersome for the needs and capability of the subsidiary. The demand for detailed data, which are often unavailable or unreliable, simply encourages halfhearted responses by subsidiary managers, who see little purpose in the planning exercise and consequently place little value on the final plan.

In too many companies the planning systems focus solely on the operational (short-term) aspects of the marketing job. Strategic and long-term planning are neglected, and for some subsidiaries in our sample the planning system was too cumbersome and time-consuming. Subsidiary marketing managers reported spending on the average 20 percent of their time working to meet home office demands for information. Some claimed, however, that nearly all their time was devoted to providing grist for the home office paper mill. In such companies simplification and rationalization would be the wisest course of action.

Rigid Evaluative Criteria. The measures used by many headquarters to evaluate performance by subsidiaries are frequently too rigid for the variation in conditions found abroad. For example, over 90 percent of the managers in our sample reported that their headquarters used the same criteria to evaluate the Brazilian subsidiary as they used for other subsidiaries around the world. Similar findings by Robbins and Stobaugh showed that 95 percent of the firms in their survey used the same standards to evaluate their domestic and foreign affiliates.[20] Regardless of the subsidiary's strategic objectives (for example, long-term growth, diversification, cash flow, or short-run profits), the same financial criteria were specified by headquarters, primarily profits, profitability, or sales revenue.

These criteria are easily circumvented, however, and when little flexibility is allowed, subsidiary management is inadvertently motivated to circumvent. American subsidiaries placed the greatest emphasis on achieving the operating targets given in the plan. The extent of resulting circumvention may be judged from Table 1, which indicates that nearly half the managers of American subsidiaries admitted to the practice of sending a "reduced" estimate to headquarters, thereby attempting to ensure easier achievement of planned goals. This figure compares with 28 percent in European firms and 17 percent in Japanese firms. Furthermore, in establishing quotas for the sales force, managers in American firms were far more inclined to set quotas that exceeded the forecast in

[20]Robbins and Stobaugh, *op. cit.*, p. 82.

the plan. The incidence of these practices was probably much higher than the reported results, but we have no reason to suspect a systematic bias by nationality. The prevalence of these practices in American subsidiaries illustrates some of the responses of subsidiary managers to performance pressures imposed by the home office. In the process the use of planning as a management tool also becomes subverted.

Inadequate Data Support for Subsidiary. Another problem relates to the failure of headquarters to gather and provide information necessary for effective planning by the subsidiary. Unexplainable lags of information often occur between headquarters and subsidiary. Moving relevant information from one subsidiary to another or from a domestic product division to an overseas subsidiary was a frequent problem noted by managers. For example, a subsidiary might be given a new product to introduce without receiving information on how the product had fared elsewhere. Some relief lies in better education of home office personnel to the realities of subsidiary life. Companies must also pay more attention to the planning of intracompany communications flows. More careful management of information should result in a flow of communications that is better coordinated with subsidiary needs.[21] This issue is discussed in detail in Chapter 5.

Subsidiary Planning System Problems

The difficulties listed in cell D (Figure 2) stem mainly from the problems of obtaining useful information and qualified people to assist in the planning process.

Scarce or Unreliable Market Data. Local market data are often unavailable, unreliable, or outdated, and the cost of primary collection is high. In the absence of sufficient trained manpower, the problem is worsened, since senior executives are forced to become more heavily involved in data collection.

Managers complain that they are constantly burdened with too

---

[21]William K. Brandt and James M. Hulbert, "Patterns of Communications in the Multinational Corporation: An Empirical Study," *Journal of International Business Studies,* Vol. 7, No. 1 (Spring 1976), pp. 57–64, and "Communication Problems in the Multinational Corporation: The Subsidiary Viewpoint," *Proceedings* of the American Marketing Association, 1975, pp. 326–330.

much information of the "wrong kind" and too little of the "right kind." However, in many of the host countries in which multinationals operate, this maxim does not apply. With the exception of subsidiaries in a small number of developed countries, the managers of subsidiaries face a dearth of any kind of information.

Data problems are even more acute if the host country is rapidly developing. Not only is the information quickly outdated, but the widespread structural changes in the economies and societies of these countries make it difficult to develop useful benchmarks for time-series projections. Similarly, the immense internal migrations and urbanization rates of the population of developing countries profoundly affect the sales potentials for certain products, services, and geographic areas.

In some cases companies attempt to solve the problem by directly basing their plans on estimates used for governmental planning. This approach may work, but in some cases it becomes little more than the blind leading the blind. The subsidiary may have a rationale for defending decisions against home office criticism, but has not improved its planning. Furthermore, this strategy is likely to work much better for companies whose products are purchased by the government sector or whose use is linked with infrastructure investments (for example, computers, telecommunication). It offers little solace to many manufacturers, who need data on industrial or consumer markets, which are generally far more difficult to obtain. Consequently, many companies face the continual problem of planning with only meager informational inputs.

Under such conditions good planning places a premium on skill, ingenuity, and flexibility. The normal response, of course, is to fall back on the most easily accessible sources of data. More ingenious approaches, however, are legion. One American subsidiary, for example, unable to find a commercial research service maintaining a consumer panel, set up its own service and sold it to noncompeting companies.

In many overseas markets, financial reporting requirements are much less demanding than in the United States, so that a subsidiary may have great difficulty obtaining even basic data on its competitors. Innovative responses to this problem are quite evident, and although a number of these practices are illegal in the United States, illegality has not discouraged the overseas perpetrators. (Perhaps the awakened concern over corporate ethics and bribery might lead to some changes here, however.) Thus solutions range from friendly discussions (swapping information with competitors), to aggressive hiring from competitors (much more easily practiced where the demand for competent managers exceeds supply), to putting competitor's employees on an unofficial payroll. .

Some of these practices are unsavory, to say the least, but it is interesting to note that more rigorous disclosure laws and establishing of trade associations (which commonly provide current industry statistics to members) would alleviate these information problems and also improve corporate morality. Concern over becoming the victim of such tactics is rampant among subsidiaries, some of which go to extreme lengths to maintain the secrecy of their own planning documents. In some cases, this goes so far as to require that *no* copies of plans remain in the country of origin, a requirement so restrictive as to lead to wondering what use the plans might then have to the subsidiary concerned.

Many subsidiaries also rely heavily on suppliers of commercial research. Two reasons appear to account for this practice. First, many subsidiaries are too small to provide economic justification for a specialized internal market research department. Second, in many host countries it is virtually impossible to find local nationals well trained in this specialty. The economics of importing talent for such purposes are clearly more favorable for a commercial research supplier than for an individual subsidiary, unless it is of considerable size.

Inadequate Information System.   Headquarters carries special responsibility for ensuring that subsidiary planning system problems stay within reasonable limits. Requirements for data must be developed to reflect both the realities of the subsidiary's environment and its manpower limitations. And wherever special projects require the development of comparable multicountry data bases, headquarters should become involved and should assume proportions of the time and budget costs. Many multinationals handle this problem through a central international department for marketing research or marketing planning.

RECOMMENDATIONS FOR IMPROVEMENT

Improving the quality of planning in the multinational enterprise requires careful consideration to the role of planning and the way in which plans are used. In our survey nearly half the chief executives of American subsidaries reported that the plan represented a commitment or a target to be met. In European and Japanese firms managers were more inclined to emphasize the benefits of planning for coordination and budgetary purposes. Among American multinationals, therefore, planning was used largely as a control mechanism.

Depending on its design and use, the planning process can serve several purposes for the firm: as a control mechanism, as a means of coordinating disparate operations, and as a stimulus to improve performance. Figure 3 presents a means-ends chain showing how the primary purpose for which planning is used also influences other decisions and activities. For example, if the plan is fundamentally a device for controlling foreign subsidiaries, the

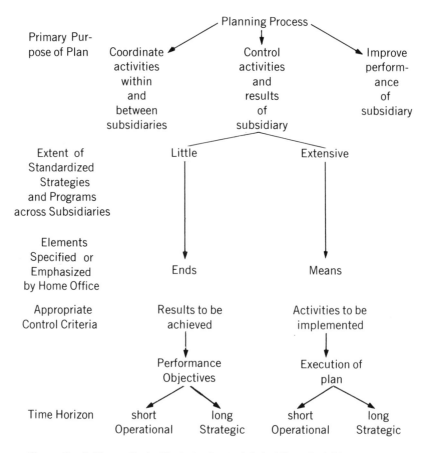

Figure 3 A Means-Ends Chain to Control Subsidiary Activities through the Planning Process

home office must decide how much to standardize the strategies and programs for its subsidiaries.[22]

By definition, greater standardization means that the home office plays a leading role in providing the content of the plan, i.e., the *means* by which the *ends* will be achieved. To be consistent, home offices therefore should evaluate the subsidiary more on the basis of how well it implements the activities set forth in the plan, either short run or long run.

Firms preferring less standardization of strategies and programs can still use the plan as a device for control. There the emphasis should focus on the *ends* instead of the *means* — i.e., what the subsidiary is expected to achieve in sales, profits, and other goals — rather than how it is supposed to reach these goals. The control criteria therefore must emphasize the attainment of the goals, whether short or long term.

A final important factor is the time perspective. Many firms, particularly American multinationals, take a short-term view of their subsidiary operations, an attitude that encourages emphasis on immediate profits. Others, for example, the Japanese, take a much longer term view. One Japanese executive described the early years of his subsidiary in Brazil as a time for a deliberate "profit-neglecting sales strategy," expressing the view that the primary objective was to build volume and share; profits would come later. (This point is elaborated in Chapter 4, page 70).

The second factor, for want of a better name, we label a "strategic versus financial orientation." In many firms we observed that planning was extremely budget oriented. Objectives were stated exclusively in terms of sales, profits, or profitability, and the content of the plan other than financial data was meager. With a strategic orientation, plans embrace a broader perspective and include a discussion of the current situation; assumptions about the future; the development of strategies and programs; a variety of objectives for market share, new product, and market development; and human resource development, to name only a few.

Our assessment of planning systems indicates that many multinationals were both short run in time perspective and very financially oriented. These attitudes, when combined with heavy intervention from headquarters, produced several consequences: (1) strategic myopia, which was likely to jeopardize long-run perfor-

---

[22]Brandt and Hulbert, *op. cit.,* 1978.

ance of the subsidiary, (2) inflexible and sometimes hostile attitudes about headquarters (and probably vice versa as well), and (3) in some cases, manipulation of plans to ensure "success" in meeting objectives and keeping home office staff from asking questions. Under such conditions these subsidiaries are at an operational and strategic disadvantage compared with their competitors. In contrast, a company emphasizing appropriate objectives, with a longer term strategic orientation, produces an environment that affords to subsidiary management greater flexibility and freedom and less concern about specifying the means to achieve objectives.

Management Changes

The paradigm in Figure 2 suggests specific recommendations for improving the planning process. First, it should be recognized that the perspectives and interests of headquarters and subsidiary managers are and should be different. Headquarters must focus on the potential and problems of the regional or worldwide market; the subsidiary must consider its markets. Both, however, need to see the planning effort as an interactive, supportive effort. This does not occur by fiat; instead it comes from careful study, training, and confidence building on both sides.

In the case of Brazil, for example, headquarters must understand that dealing with an inflation rate of 30 to 50 percent a year requires different tactics from those which might be appropriate in the parent country. Similarly, it should realize that heavy government participation in business does not inevitably imply a socialist political posture.

Subsidiary managers must recognize that, even in turbulent markets, planning for the future is a key task. Acceptance of this idea among top subsidiary managers makes it easier to push the concept down through the organization to the point where all managers are involved in the process. Subsidiary managers should also recognize how their operation fits into the long-range corporate plan, so that even if funding is drawn away from their subsidiary, they will understand better how this action is integrated into the company's global strategy.

The results also suggest that headquarters in many firms needs to adopt a broader perspective and more flexible attitude. Planning has often become a straitjacket from which subsidiary managers spend too much time trying to engineer Houdini-like escapes. The time would be better spent developing appropriate medium- and long-term strategic objectives and providing the kinds of support necessary to achieve them. This requires training for middle and lower level managers, programs to familiarize home office staff with subsidiary environments, and a more flexible attitude toward the strategic situation of particular subsidiaries. Whereas certain approaches may be appropriate for a mature subsidiary, a fledging operation demands a different system. In sum, multinational firms must learn to apply for foreign markets the same portfolio approaches being used increasingly at home.[23]

Improving the Planning System

The practice of running subsidiaries "by the numbers" without sufficient regard for business conditions is perhaps the primary contraint on more effective planning. The strong financial perspective of headquarters often leads to a myopic view of foreign operations. With competition for many products becoming truly global, foreign subsidiaries become as integral to the worldwide strategy as domestic operations are to domestic strategies. Regarding the foreign affiliates in this manner reduces the chances that accounting considerations will overwhelm more critical strategic issues.

Indiscriminate reliance on financial data is often dangerous for a multinational firm planning and evaluating its subsidiary operations. Decisions on issues such as transfer prices, tax allowances, or depreciation charges are generally *not* made with the objective of attaining a fair and reasonable portrayal of subsidiary operations.[24] Yet these decisions certainly affect the subsidiary's profitability. When the time arrives to review subsidiary performance, how these decisions were made is all too easily forgotten. Thus, in the multinational, as elsewhere, there is a strong argument that accounting systems used for tax or even custodial purposes do not adequately support various management decisions — perhaps one factor in the widespread practice among subsidiaries of keeping several sets of books.

There is also a strong case for making the planning system as

[23]See, for example, George Day "Alternative Portfolio Strategies," *Journal of Marketing,* Vol. 41 (April 1977), pp. 29–38.
[24]Robbins and Stobaugh, *op. cit.*

simple as possible to meet the needs of both subsidiary and head-quarters. Unfortunately, in many firms the opposite thinking rules: Attempts are made to collect and analyze data that are simply not available, or pressure to build uniform cross-country data bases means that excessive time and effort are expended by all subsidiaries primarily to meet home office requirements.

Certainly, obvious benefits are derived by the use of identical planning formats on a regional or worldwide basis, but the expectations of detail and sophistication within the format should be considered on an "as needed" basis. Home office attempts to assess long-range potentials for particular new products, for example, should be organized and dealt with on a project basis, instead of placing an excessive burden on the normal planning structure. With a more selective approach, subsidiaries can more reasonably be put on notice that certain kinds of data should be collected and stored on a regular basis.

Flexibility should also be built into the planning system in another way. To move away from the strict reliance on rigid, even uniform, financial criteria for evaluation, Robbins and Stobaugh recommend that the annual plan itself become the basis for evaluation.[25] Under such a system the subsidiary would be evaluated on the basis of how well it achieved its strategic objective along the lines stipulated in the plan; there are important provisos, however. The plans must be appropriate, and excessive pressures should be avoided.

SUMMARY

In this chapter we have reviewed the planning practices of multinational subsidiaries and their relations with headquarters during the planning process. We examined the planning problems experienced by multinationals, using a simple paradigm to classify problems on two dimensions, whether the problems arise from headquarters or the subsidiary, and whether they result from the planning system itself or are caused by the managers involved in running the system. Finally, several recommendations for improving the system were presented.

Defining the planning responsibility in a multinational operation

[25]*Ibid.*, pp. 87–88.

is a difficult task. To develop and execute global plans and strategies necessarily implies an important role for headquarters and close cooperation between executives in the home office and its subsidiaries. Unfortunately, in many companies we observed an adversarial relation. Some stresses and difficulties are inevitable; unless tensions are checked, however, the discussions can deteriorate into chaos, diverting into intrafirm disputes substantial energies that might be better employed against competitors.

Some authors on international management appear to take the position that the task of running a multinational firm can be reduced to a small group of managers in New York, London, or Tokyo pulling strings that result in global marketing warfare. Nothing could be further from the truth. Just as domestic competitive battles are fought at the corner supermarket or over the purchasing agent's desk at the local plant, the plans of the most ambitious multinational are reduced to the search for the next customer and the next order.

No matter how sophisticated home office management and its data banks may become, they can never be self-sufficient in plotting and executing marketing strategy. Moreover, subsidiary management must also recognize that the days when they could pursue their own paths are likewise gone. To derive full benefit from multinational operations demands synergistic relationships between headquarters and its subsidiaries — antipathy must yield to acceptance of the need for cooperation.

Thus, despite the effort and time devoted to the development of coordinated global marketing strategy, multinationals must rely on their subsidiaries, if strategies are to be successful. In many subsidiaries, however, planning efforts remain limited, if not crude, and hampered by a variety of problems which need not concern domestic management, at least in American multinationals. In other companies, subsidiary planning systems are highly refined — in some cases far too refined for the subsidiaries, who are supposed to contribute to and benefit from the system.

Planning should be a major factor in increasing the degree of integration and coordination in the multinational. Yet our conclusions are that most of the problems lie with people instead of planning systems. Until managers change, many of the problems may persist indefinitely. As the multinational firm has evolved, it has become a much more closely linked entity than was true in earlier days. There is today a much greater need for close integration of the firm's activities, particularly with respect to the home office and its subsidiaries. Perhaps a new generation of managers will be necessary before truly cooperative and integrative home office/subsidiary relations develop. In the meantime, many existing managers will have to change their attitudes considerably if progress is to be made.

Chapter 4

Formulating Subsidiary Strategy

The pressures imposed by operational problems often leave little time for serious thought about the broader strategic issues that are crucial determinants of business success.

The importance of these strategic decisions at the subsidiary level should be evident. Although a global strategic perspective is always valuable,[1] it is at the level of the subsidiaries' products and markets that global corporations joust in the battle for growth and profits. This is the level at which the business giants of Europe, the United States, and Japan shed their cloaks of corporate respectability and enter the fray to battle in earnest.

It is also at the subsidiary level that the best-laid global plots of remote home office managers stand or fall on the performance of their subsidiary personnel. Similarly, this is the level at which reticent, ignorant, or insensitive home office management can trammel the best efforts of subsidiary executives. If the organization structures, planning systems, and communication channels of the multinational are not functioning effectively, they can jeopardize the success of the best strategies and harm the performance of the company as a whole.

A distinction must be made between strategies and plans. In this chapter, when we deal with strategy, we focus on the formulation

[1]"To a Global Car," *Business Week,* November 20, 1978, pp. 102–113.

of business objectives and on the basic resource allocation decisions necessary to attain those objectives. Plans are much more embracing, and include (usually) historical information; forecasts; assumptions; statements of objectives, strategies, programs, and budgets; and a means of monitoring the results.

OBJECTIVES, STRATEGIES, AND PROGRAMS

Because the terms objective, strategy, and program often carry many meanings, we begin by clarifying the use of each in this chapter. "Objectives" refers to a state, a result, which the company's management wishes to achieve. We should distinguish between strategic objectives and operational objectives or targets. By strategic objectives we refer to the overall primary objectives being sought for a business over a given period. To make this objective tangible, it must be translated into a specific numerical target to be achieved — this we term the operational objective. It is also helpful to distinguish short-term and long-term objectives. The former is an objective we expect to attain within the operational planning period (one or two years in most companies); the latter is related to the company's strategic planning horizon — a five- to ten-year period in most companies.

Choice of the appropriate strategic objective at a given point in time is crucial. Seeking profits too early can jeopardize the growth of the business; seeking increases in share of a mature market can prove expensive. The following matrix (Table 1) illustrates the kinds of objectives that might be formulated for a new product.

Linked to these business objectives are a variety of supporting functional objectives. For example, the production objectives

Table 1
Sample Objectives Matrix

	Time Horizon	
Type	*Short Term*	*Long Term*
Strategic	Increase market share	Attain dominant market share
Operational	Attain 10 percent of total market one year after introduction	Our share will be 150 percent of the combined shares of the next two competitors at the end of year 4

might be (1) to expand pilot production to X units per day by the end of year 1 and (2) to achieve a reject rate of 1 percent or less. Marketing objectives might include attaining distribution in 50 percent of retail outlets by the end of year 1; advertising objectives might include attaining 60 percent awareness in the target market in the same time period.

"Strategy" deals with the ways in which resources, e.g., investment funds, plant capacity, or human resources, are allocated to achieve the strategic objective(s) of the business. At the level of business strategy in the subsidiary, we deal only with general allocations, which in turn should be supported by a consistent set of functional strategies. Thus our overall strategy may be to achieve customer acceptance of the new product by heavy advertising of certain product features while rapidly expanding distribution in high-volume outlets. A supporting sales strategy might be:

- Devote 20 percent of total customer contact time to new product in year 1.
- Increase frequency of calls to high-volume outlets by 30 percent; reduce call frequency to low-volume outlets.
- Stress superior features, retail and wholesale deals, and heavy advertising schedule — distribute pop material.

Similar strategies may also be developed in advertising, finance, production, and other areas.

The final element in the trilogy (objectives, strategies, and programs) is to establish programs to ensure implementation of the chosen strategies. Programs should specify who does what, by when, and with what resources. Unless the strategy itself is clearly defined and described, there is no basis on which to develop programs.

Choice of Strategic Objectives

Selecting the strategic objective for a product line or business division presents a crucial decision for any manager. Should he or she strive to build market share and sales volume, improve its level of profits, or generate greater cash flows that can be used by other product divisions or other subsidiaries in the multinational corporation? Ideally the manager desires all the preceding goals. Unfortunately, in the short run some trade-off is necessary. For example, building market share can require substantial investments in time and money, which in the near term will adversely affect profits and cash flow. On the other hand, choosing to maximize cash flow implies an unwillingness to invest heavily in the new capacity, which can limit potential growth of the business.

Entry Objectives

Reasons for the initial decision to manufacture overseas are never easy to identify. Beclouded by history and buried in complex patterns of political and financial pressures and sheer entrepreneurial will, motives are difficult to classify and evaluate. Brooke and Remmers, for example, found that "defensive" motives predominated. Companies found themselves faced with the necessity of protecting existing foreign markets against a variety of threats, including such factors as tariff barriers, import controls, rising nationalism, or competitive activities.[2] Other companies stated more aggressive rationales, including more profitable uses of underemployed resources and desire to capitalize on global opportunities. In our survey, subsidiary chief executives stressed the desire to expand the market for their companies' products; and although other reasons were offered, this was given most frequently.[3] In any case, whether the motive was defensive or aggressive, during the earlier periods of the subsidiary's operation we would expect growth objectives to dominate. This objective was what we observed for Brazilian subsidiaries.

Current Objectives

To identify the strategic objectives being following in Brazil, we asked managers to specify the principal marketing goals for their major product lines during the current planning period. Although many executives found it difficult to articulate their objectives, four categories of goals were identified (Table 2).

Most chief executives were concerned with market penetration — securing larger market shares for existing products. Nearly half the managers stated their goals in this way. If we add sales growth, a less specific objective, we find that nearly two-thirds specified their objectives in terms of market penetration.

[2]Michael Z. Brooke and H. Lee Remmers, *The Strategy of Multinational Enterprise* (New York: American Elsevier Publishers, 1970), pp. 224–238.
[3]William K. Brandt and James M. Hulbert, *A Empresa Multinacional* (Rio de Janeiro: Zahar Editores, 1977), Chapter 2.

Table 2
Choice of Strategic Objective

	Diversi-fication	Market Penetration	Sales Growth	Profit and Other	Total
Number of companies	11	23	9	6	49
Percent of sample	22%	47%	18%	12%	100%

Another pathway to growth involves the development of new products or markets, an alternative we label diversification. One out of five executives claimed that this was his principal objective. Several noted that competitive pressures were forcing them to search for new products and markets, a condition mentioned most often by makers of consumer products. In the case of Brazil, an increasingly discriminating customer was also driving this change. As one manager commented: "We need to find new and better products to satisfy today's consumer. She no longer accepts the poor quality and limited assortment we offered her in the past."

Although three out of four subsidiaries were evaluated by their home offices on the basis of profit performance, only one out of twelve mentioned profits as the primary objective. Some managers noted that profits are important, but this objective was mentioned in conjunction with some other objective. Peter Drucker has argued for decades that profits do not constitute a useful, operational objective;[4] however, the apparent lack of correspondence between strategic objectives pursued and evaluative criteria used is surprising. We return to this topic in Chapter 6, where we illustrate how the inflexibility of control procedures encourages this inconsistency.

Subsidiary Characteristics and Choice of Strategic Objectives

Choice of objectives and strategies is constrained by resources available and those which may be acquired — from within the multinational as a whole or from outside the company. Thus we should expect to find some association between a subsidiary's

[4]Peter F. Drucker, *Management: Tasks, Responsibilities, Practices* (New York: Harper & Row, 1974).

strategic objectives and its other characteristics. Table 1 in Appendix B shows the results of our analysis of these relationships.

Japanese subsidiaries were the most recent arrivals in our Brazilian sample and tended to favor sales growth objectives. It is notable that Japanese managers specified sales growth, since this corresponds with their prevailing export strategy.[5] Sales volume above all else appeared to be the prime concern for many Japanese managers; in their view, profits will come in time. One manager summarized this philosophy in the following way:

Sometimes we engage in what we call "profit-neglecting sales strategies." This means that sales volume is stressed rather than profits or market share. Because of our lifetime employment system in Japan, labor in effect becomes a fixed cost. The only way to maintain reasonable profits in this situation is through greater efficiency — more output per worker. Consequently, sometimes we must reduce our profit margins in favor of greater volume. You might say that our profits result as much from concern over production efficiencies as from profit margins.

Several significant relationships were observed between the company's strategic objectives and its organizational structure. For firms pursuing penetration objectives, customer research is the key resource needed to segment and develop their markets effectively. It is not surprising, therefore, that 95 percent of the companies with these objectives also had their own market research departments. For firms seeking other goals, only 57 percent maintained such a group internally. Thus, those companies pursuing market share also organized themselves to facilitate achievement of their objectives.

A related finding shows that companies adopting a product manager system were more disposed toward profit objectives. In this instance we conjecture that the decentralization of responsibility to product managers serves to focus greater attention on profits instead of sales and market share. Although product managers seldom have much direct authority to influence profits, they are often held responsible for bottom-line results.

Finally, if the marketing department — instead of R&D, engineering, production, or some other group — was given responsi-

---

[5]For further discussion of the strategies followed by multinationals of different nationalities, see W. K. Brandt and J. M. Hulbert, "Market Strategies of American, European and Japanese Multinational Subsidiaries," paper presented to the Academy of International Business, Fontainbleau, France, July 1975.

bility for new product development, the company tended to stress diversification objectives. Although we do not know whether more or less innovation results from this structure, it does appear to influence the firm's overall growth strategy.

In the long run, the need for strategic changes may well prompt changes in organizational structure. In the short run, however, the findings observed in Brazil demonstrate a significant relationship between strategic objectives and organization structure. This result may seem surprising in view of the fact that the analysis was limited to characteristics of the subsidiary company and did not include the parent's characteristics.

Two points are important here. First, there is no doubt that the subsidiary may avail itself of a variety of parent resources in developing its objectives and executing its strategies. However, some of these resources are much more transferable than others, and the interchange is therefore selective and constrained, as we see when we further explore this issue later in the chapter. Second, the most important implication is to recognize that feasible strategies for the subsidiary are bounded by resource availability and organization structure. Subsidiary managers who expect to develop new and innovative strategies must clearly plan for the requisite organizational development over the longer term, and must be prepared to combat shorter term thinking if they expect to execute strategies successfully.

Emphasis of Current Strategy

Although most managers are familiar with the term strategy, its meaning and usage in planning differ dramatically. As we have noted, clear-cut statements of strategy are often missing from marketing plans, and many managers find it difficult to articulate their strategies.

We attempted to determine the emphasis of the company's current strategy by asking subsidiary marketing managers which decisions were most critical in helping them achieve their objectives. The decision areas included sales force, advertising, sales promotion, distribution, pricing, new market development, and new product development.

Table 3 indicates that European and American firms emphasized sales force decisions, whereas the Japanese focused more on pricing and developing new markets and products. The results for the Japanese firms seem consistent with their objectives and general market position: Their relatively small size and limited product lines forced them to expand into new markets and to broaden their product lines. And their low-price strategy, which proved so effective for export development in the past, appears to be a central thrust of their expansion into overseas manufacturing.

HEADQUARTERS GUIDANCE AND SUBSIDIARY STRATEGY

Managing a multinational enterprise to achieve corporate objectives requires some degree of integration and cohesion among foreign subsidiaries. The practices adopted by headquarters to attain the desired level of integration differ dramatically from firm to firm; we examine the issues of control of the multinational in more depth in Chapter 6. However, for the purposes of guiding and controlling subsidiary business and market strategy, two broad patterns may be identified.

The first is a pattern of hierarchical authority by headquarters. In these cases, home office decisions are imposed on subsidiary managers, who are responsible for their execution.[6] Centralizing

Table 3
Emphasis of Current Strategy by Nationality of Parent Company

Decision Area	Nationality of Parent Company		
	American	European	Japanese
Sales force	38%[a]	58%	0%
Sales promotion	17	33	17
Advertising	33	17	17
Pricing	30	21	50
Distribution	17	21	17
New markets	25	17	50
New products	29	25	33
Number of cases	(24)	(24)	(6)

[a]Table should be read: 38 percent of American subsidiaries reported that sales force decisions were the first or the second in importance for achieving the marketing objective.

[6]John Child, "Organization Structures and Strategies of Control: A Replication of the Aston Study," *Administrative Science Quarterly*, Vol. 17, (1972), pp. 163–177.

decision making limits the autonomy of subsidiary management and establishes authority for many day-to-day decisions at the regional or headquarters level.

The second is a pattern of integration of global activities through standardized marketing strategies and programs. Although this pattern is the focus of extensive research in multinational marketing,[7] the use of standardized programs may or may not be associated directly with centralization, as defined above.

In some firms, standardization obviates the need for direct involvement in decision making implied by centralization. In others, standardized programs complement the procedures adopted by headquarters to maintain a tight rein over subsidiary decisions.

Much research has been done in an attempt to identify how much autonomy subsidiary management enjoys with respect to strategy decisions. For example, it is alleged that subsidiary managers enjoy considerable discretion in making marketing decisions, especially when compared with their decision-making

[7]R. J. Aylmer, "Who Makes Marketing Decisions in the Multinational Firm?" *Journal of Marketing*, Vol. 34 (October 1970), pp. 25–30.

Robert Buzzell, "Can You Standardize Multinational Marketing?" *Harvard Business Review*, Vol. 46, No. 6 (November–December 1968), pp. 102–113.

S. Watson Dunn, (ed.), *International Handbook of Advertising*, (New York: McGraw-Hill, 1964).

———, "The Case Study Approach in Cross-Cultural Research," *Journal of Marketing Research*, Vol. 3, No. 1 (February 1966), pp. 26–31.

———, "Effect of National Identity on Multinational Promotion Strategy in Europe," *Journal of Marketing*, Vol. 40, No. 4 (October 1976), pp. 50–57.

Erik Elender, "International Advertisers Must Devise Universal Ads," *Advertising Age*, November 27, 1961, pp. 91–96.

Arthur C. Fatt, "The Danger of 'Local' Advertising," *Journal of Marketing*, Vol. 31, No. 1 (January 1967), pp. 61–62.

Warren J. Keegan, "Multinational Product Planning: Strategic Alternatives," *Journal of Marketing*, Vol. 33, No. 1 (January 1969), pp. 58–62.

John K. Ryans, Jr., and James H. Donnelly, Jr., "Standardized Global Advertising: A Call as Yet Unanswered," *Journal of Marketing*, Vol. 33, No. 3 (April 1969), pp. 57–60.

Ralph Z. Sorenson, and Ulrich E. Wiechmann, "How Multinationals View Marketing Standardization," *Harvard Business Review*, Vol. 53 (May–June 1975), pp. 38–167.

Ulrich E. Wiechmann, "Integrating Multinational Marketing Activities," *Columbia Journal of World Business*, Vol. 9, No. 4 (Winter 1974), pp. 7–16.

Yoram Wind, Susan Douglas, and Howard Perlmutter, "Guidelines for Developing International Marketing Strategies," *Journal of Marketing*, Vol. 37, No. 2 (April 1973), pp. 14–23.

power in areas such as finance and production.[8] Within marketing, however, the amount of discretion is related to the type of decision being made. In most companies, product-related decisions, such as quality and composition, brand name, packaging, and add-delete decisions, are tightly controlled by the home office.[9] For distribution, price, and promotional decisions, however, more autonomy has generally been observed, although the practice varies greatly by company and industry. Little research is available for industrial or consumer durable products, but among nondurables, such as cosmetics, soaps, pharmaceuticals, and soft drinks, standardized approaches are quite common. Food products, however, tend to be more culture bound and therefore less adaptable to standardized programs.[10]

Our research concentrated on the role of home office as perceived by subsidiary management, and attempted to measure the amount and type of strategic guidance received from headquarters. This approach is consistent with the subsidiary perspective, since the subsidiary manager may be unaware of whether headquarters assistance is standardized across markets or developed for his particular subsidiary.

Extent of Home Office Guidance

The subsidiaries in our survey received most guidance from the parent company in the product-related elements of the marketing mix: product specification, brand name, and package decisions (see Table 4). In contrast, less guidance was received for promotion and price decisions: less than one-fourth the companies claimed to receive guidance in these areas. Although response bias may have reduced the absolute percentages reported, the rankings and levels of guidance correspond closely with previous research.[11]

---

[8]Robert J. Alsegg, *Control Relationships Between American Corporations and Their European Subsidiaries* (New York: American Management Association, 1971).
William K. Brandt, and James M. Hulbert, *A Empresa Multinacional No Brasil op. cit.*
[9]Sorenson and Wiechmann, *op. cit.*
[10]Dunn, "The Case Study Approach . . . ," *op. cit.*
[11]Aylmer, *op. cit.*
Wiechmann, *op. cit.*
Wind, Douglas, and Perlmutter, *op. cit.*

Table 4

Subsidiaries Receiving Help from Home Office for Major Decision Areas

Marketing Decision Area	Proportion Receiving Help
Product	
Product design specifications	45%
Brand name	47
Packaging design	32
Promotion	
Basic advertising message	25
Sales promotion ideas	23
Sales force management	13
Pricing	
Pricing guidelines	17
Number of cases	(53)

Influence on Extent of Guidance

The explanatory variables investigated are grouped into two categories: those describing the parent company and those pertaining to the subsidiary.

Parent Company Variables. Parent company variables include type of industry, nationality of the parent company, volume of worldwide sales, proportion of sales outside the home market, and number of countries with manufacturing subsidiaries.

Although the differences are not statistically significant, the type of industry or product class seems to be associated with home office guidance (see Table 5). Manufacturers of consumer-packaged goods received the least guidance,[12] followed by manufacturers of motor vehicles, and electrical and telecommunications products. Pharmaceutical subsidiaries received much more direction from their headquarters, particularly in promotion and pricing, areas in which other industries tended to be more autonomous.[13]

Neither nationality of the parent company nor its size as measured by worldwide sales revenues revealed any important rela-

[12]Eighty percent of the packaged-goods companies in the sample manufactured food products.
[13]Office equipment companies also received more support from headquarters, but the small sample size for this industry limits the reliability of this finding.

Table 5
Home Office Guidance by Industry

Industry	Amount of Guidance[a]			Number of Cases
	None or Little	Moderate	Considerable	
Consumer-packaged goods	60%	20%	20%	10
Pharmaceuticals and chemicals	25%	42%	33%	12
Motor vehicles and major components	47%	40%	13%	15
Electrical and telecommunications	50%	30%	20%	10
Office equipment	0	100%	0	3
Textiles	33%	67%	0	3

[a]*"None or little" means home office help was received for none or one of the seven decisions areas in Table 4; "moderate," two or three decision areas; "considerable," four to seven decision areas.*

tionship to the extent of headquarters guidance. The Europeans provided more advertising assistance and the Americans more pricing guidelines, but the differences are not statistically significant. The proportion of sales outside the home market also had little effect on marketing support from the home office. This result contradicts Aylmer's finding of a "fairly strong relationship" between the percentage of international sales and the frequency of higher level decisions,[14] but with only nine firms in Aylmer's sample, his results are not statistically significant.

Another measure of foreign involvement, the number of countries in which manufacturing subsidiaries are located, showed an inverted-U effect in its relationship with headquarters guidance (see Table 6). Firms operating in fewer than sixteen countries offered very little assistance, whereas those with sixteen to thirty subsidiaries provided substantial assistance. Above this number of markets, however, somewhat less guidance was offered. This finding corresponds with the Sorenson and Wiechmann thesis that as firms become truly multinational, they develop standardized processes — for example, planning guides and formats and control procedures — which reduce the need for standardized programs.[15]

[14]Aylmer, *op. cit.*
[15]Sorenson and Wiechmann, *op. cit.*

Table 6
Home Office Guidance by Number of Overseas Subsidiaries[a]

Number of Subsidiaries	Amount of Guidance			Number of Cases
	None or Little	Moderate	Considerable	
Less than 16	75%	17%	8%	22
16–30	17%	33%	50%	19
More than 30	39%	46%	15%	12

[a]*"Number of overseas subsidiaries" represents the number of countries in which the parent company has manufacturing facilities, wholly or partially owned.*

Subsidiary Variables. Five subsidiary characteristics were cross-classified with guidance measures to determine whether characteristics of the subsidiary itself influenced the type or extent of direction received from headquarters. The variables included subsidiary sales volume, subsidiary sales volume as a percent of world sales, type of organizational structure, use of product managers in marketing, and presence of an internal marketing research department.

No important relationships were observed between subsidiary size, measured in absolute and relative terms, and the level of guidance. Although larger subsidiaries (those with sales over $100 million) tended to receive less guidance, the differences were not significant. Similarly, subsidiaries whose sales revenues were large, as a percentage of worldwide sales (over 6 percent), tended to receive less guidance, as did subsidiaries with less than 1 percent of world sales. Neither of the two organizational variables was significantly associated with home office assistance.

The presence of an internal department for marketing research did have some association with home office assistance. For six of the seven decision areas, subsidiaries without a marketing research department (26 percent) received more guidance from the home office. Although the results are not statistically significant, they suggest that a marketing research department at the subsidiary reduces the need for guidance that headquarters might otherwise provide. That the presence of a marketing research department is really a surrogate for subsidiary sophistication might be a reasonable hypothesis, but the data do not provide an answer. We do know that almost all subsidiaries in the sample with sales exceeding $50 million had research departments, but as already observed, size of subsidiary is not closely associated with home office guidance.

Effect of Subsidiary Strategy

Standardized programs are designed both to aid the subsidiary in achieving its objectives and to provide a means of control over its activities. Thus the types of guidance offered should correspond in some logical way to the marketing strategies pursued by the subsidiary. Here we examine the fit between subsidiary objectives and strategies, and the types of marketing assistance received from headquarters.

The results shown in Table 7 demonstrate that subsidiaries pursuing penetration objectives (as defined earlier in the chapter) received significantly less home office direction than those following diversification objectives. To achieve penetration objectives, local market information was crucial. It is not surprising, therefore, that these subsidiaries were also more inclined to have internal departments for marketing research.

Diversification objectives, whether they involve developing new products or new markets, represented much riskier directions of growth.[16] A predictable response to increased risk is greater home

Table 7

Home Office Guidance by Strategic Objective of Subsidiary

	Amount of Guidance		
Strategic Objective	None or Little	Moderate or Considerable	Number of Cases
Penetration[a]	82%	18%	28
Diversification	14%	86%	7
Profit	50%	50%	14

[a]*Subsidiaries pursuing penetration objectives are significantly more likely to receive less guidance. (Value of chi-square = 5.01, with one degree of freedom, significant at the $p < .05$ level.)*

[16]H. Igor Ansoff, *Corporate Strategy* (New York: McGraw-Hill, 1965).
A. D. Chandler, *Strategy and Structure* (Cambridge, Mass.: M.I.T. Press, 1962).

office involvement, as was observed. Furthermore, since many subsidiaries in Brazil lacked adequate facilities for new product development, much of the guidance was essential for introducing innovations.

Subsidiaries with profit objectives were probably under substantial pressure from the home office to increase short-term profits. This concern apparently encouraged greater marketing assistance to ensure that the goals were met. The trade-off between long- and short-term profits was a major point of contention in many subsidiaries. Numerous instances were cited to illustrate how meeting short-run objectives to satisfy headquarters had greatly reduced the potential for profits three to five years hence.

In terms of types of guidance received from the home office, Table 8 provides little support for the product-promotion dichotomy used by Keegan.[17] However, a relationship does appear between strategic objectives and the amount of support received. Subsidiaries pursuing penetration objectives received less help in both product and promotional decisions. These firms received more direction with pricing decisions, a crucial element in achieving market penetration.[18] Subsidiaries with other objectives received more guidance from the home office, but there were no material differences among the types of support.

Table 8

Amount of Home Office Guidance for Product and Promotional Decisions by Strategic Objective of Subsidiary

Strategic Objective	Promotional Guidance		Product Guidance		Number of Cases
	None or Little	Moderate or Considerable	None or Little	Moderate or Considerable	
Penetration[a]	75%	25%	79%	21%	28
Diversification	14%	86%	43%	57%	7
Profit	36%	64%	43%	57%	14

[a]*Subsidiaries with penetration objectives are significantly less likely to receive promotion-related guidance (chi-square = 5.22, 1 d.f., p < .05) or product-related guidance (chi-square = 3.29, 1 d.f., p < .10).*

[17]Keegan, *op. cit.*
[18]*Perspectives on Experience*, Boston Consulting Group, 1968.

Besides trying to match marketing objectives and home office guidance, we also attempted to relate the type of support received to the strategic emphasis being followed by the subsidiary. Managers were asked to rank the strategic decision areas which were most crucial in achieving their objectives. These decision areas corresponded closely with those for home office guidance. We wished to learn, for example, whether a subsidiary that relied heavily on its sales force was also more inclined to receive guidance in this area. The results of these cross tabulations are disappointing, partly because of interviewer and/or questionnaire problems. It is plausible, however, that many multinationals have not yet coordinated their home office guidance with the strategies being pursued by individual subsidiaries. A correlation between marketing objectives and the amount of help received was evident, but this relationship did not carry over to the types of help most needed to reach those objectives.

SUBSIDIARY PERFORMANCE

As suggested earlier, measurement of subsidiary performance is a controversial issue. There is little consensus on appropriate measures and, in many companies, little consistency between performance objectives and control criteria (see Chapter 6). Furthermore, even within a particular company, accounting idiosyncracies can distort the measurement of performance in ways not fully understood by all participants in the evaluation process. Finally, as a multinational becomes more globally integrated in its planning and strategy, it becomes less helpful to view individual subsidiaries as independent profit centers with profit maximization as an objective. In fact, global optimization is quite likely to mean that individual subsidiaries cannot pursue local optima. Similar consequences will often derive from adopting portfolio approaches to strategic planning.

However, an attempt to measure and evaluate subsidiary performance must be made, not only by companies themselves but also by other interested bodies — host governments, home governments, and such international institutions as the United Nations. Although the process is fraught with difficulty, it is far from futile. Careful analysis of available information can help in assessing the direction and magnitude of possible biases, and may provide valuable insights into subsidiary economic performance.

Two issues should be clearly separated and defined. The first involves the question of whether or not profit (the most commonly used criterion) is an appropriate measure for subsidiary performance. At the risk of oversimplification, we conclude that generally it is not — certainly not when used alone. We develop this issue in more depth in Chapters 6 and 7.

The second issue considers the extent to which profits *reported* by multinational subsidiaries are of any use to outsiders, be they competitors, potential investors, regulators, or researchers. We discuss this issue in the following section.

Assessing Reported Subsidiary Profitability[19]

It is sometimes argued that figures attempting to depict the profitability of a multinational subsidiary should not be taken seriously.[20] Gross distortions of reported profits have been identified,[21] both understatement and overstatement being possible, usually depending upon taxation issues.

Brandt and Giddy present an attempt to deal with six sources of possible distortion.[22] These include high nominal interest rates, distorted royalty payments, unjustified management fees, transfer pricing of intrafirm sales, overvaluation of subsidiary assets, and misleading accounting practices. The procedure must be applied on a country-by-country basis and results only in estimates of aggregate distortions (meaning that individual companies may be

[19]This section relies heavily on the work of Brandt and Giddy, *viz.* William K. Brandt and Ian H. Giddy, "On Comparing the Profitability of Domestic and Foreign Firms," Working Paper No. 85A, Columbia University Graduate School of Business, September 1978.
[20]Raymond Vernon, *Storm over the Multinationals* (Cambridge, Mass.: Harvard University Press, 1977), p. 156. For similar criticisms see Michael Z. Brooke and H. Lee Remmers, *The Strategy of Multinational Enterprise* (New York: Elsevier, 1970), pp. 213–233; and Sidney Robbins and Robert Stobaugh, *Money in the Multinational Enterprise* (New York: Basic Books, 1973), Chapter 8.
[21]Ronald Muller, "The Multinational Corporation and the Underdevelopment of the Third World," in *The Political Economy of Development and Underdevelopment,* Charles K. Wilber (ed.) (New York: Random House, 1975). A classic study is Constantine V. Viatsos, *Intercompany Income Distribution and Transnational Enterprises* (Oxford, England: Clarendon Press, 1974).
[22]Brandt and Giddy, *op. cit.*

quite different). Furthermore, substantial amounts of data are required, but most of these are available from secondary sources. In the case of Brazil, Brandt and Giddy conclude that the maximum possible bias is small and that no serious distortion of subsidiary profits has occurred.[23]

Profitability Comparison

Table 9 shows the profitability, as measured by return on assets and return on investment (capital), of foreign and domestic firms operating in Brazil.

The figures represent calculations from a compilation of financial information on the five hundred largest private firms in Brazil for the years 1973 and 1974. A private publication, roughly equiv-

Table 9

Profit Performance of the Five Hundred Largest Private Firms by Nationality of Controlling Interest, 1974

Nationality	Mean Return[a] on Total Assets (percent)	Mean Return[a] on Equity Investment (percent)	Number of Firms
Brazilian	11.8	27.5*	260
Foreign	10.7	22.6*	218
North American	11.7	24.5	103
European	9.4	17.9	77
Japanese	12.4	35.3	17
Latin American	12.2	30.4	9
Joint ventures	9.2	16.4	12
Total (all firms)	11.3	25.4	478

[a]net return on total assets and on equity investment refers to pretax net profits as a percentage of total reported assets and equity (including retained earnings), respectively.

*Mean difference between domestic and foreign companies significant at the p < .05 level.

SOURCE: Original data compiled from Brasil Exame: Os Melhores e Os Maiores (São Paulo: Editora Abril, Setembro 1975), pp. 58–77.

[23]Ibid., p. 13.

alent to the *Fortune 500* publication in the United States, is the source of the principal data.[24] Comparisons of the estimates with other sources affirmed the general reliability of the data.

The nationality of each firm was determined by the locus of controlling interest in the Brazilian firm, either as foreign controlled or domestically controlled. Joint ventures included only those firms with substantial investment from two or more nationalities. For example, a firm owned by two U.S. companies was treated as "North American," not as a "joint venture."

In contrast to the common notion that foreign subsidiaries earn far greater profits than do domestic firms, Table 9 reveals little difference between the two groups. Profits as a percent of total assets (return on assets) differed by the statistically insignificant amount of 0.9 percentage points. The mean return on equity for domestic firms (27.5 percent) was actually significantly above the comparable figure for foreign subsidiaries (22.6 percent), although the difference narrows if joint ventures are removed from the sample. On the basis of this cursory comparison, at least, the data offer no evidence that foreign firms earn systematically higher profits than do domestic ones.[25]

MANAGING SUBSIDIARY OBJECTIVES AND STRATEGIES

It might seem presumptuous to develop any general recommendations or even guidelines in such areas as objectives and strategies. Nonetheless, some useful ideas have emerged from the study.

Selectivity and Strategy

A central tenet of all marketing is the necessity for disaggregation of markets into segments. Only if such disaggregation processes

---

[24]*Brasil Exame: Os Melhores e Os Maiores* (São Paulo: Editora Abril, September 1975), pp. 58–77.

[25]This finding is supported by that of an independent study by Carlos Von Doellinger and Leonardo C. Cavalcanti, *Empresas Multinacionals na Industra Brasileira* (Rio de Janeiro: IPEA/INPES, 1975). The reader is of course aware that bland profitability figures, even if accurate, do not necessarily represent a valid comparison. In particular, they do not show the relative riskiness of earnings of foreign and domestic firms.

fail to yield substantial differences in customer wants, distribution channels, or other factors can subsequent reaggregation into larger elements be justified.

From a broader perspective, it is completely antithetical to this philosophy to approach foreign markets with an a priori *decision* to standardize marketing programs across countries. Because there are obvious economies in doing so, an a priori *intention* to standardize where possible is justifiable. However, the decision to do so should be based on careful analysis of the foreign market being considered. The history of international marketing contains countless examples of successful standardized programs, yet it often conceals more than it reveals. For example, products often perceived as being standardized — for example, detergents and toothpastes — are routinely reformulated (while retaining the same brand) to meet the demands and characteristics of particular markets. And unless the reader jumps to the conclusion that such modifications pertain only to consumer goods, changing technical specifications and standards, and different distribution channels have led to analogous modifications to industrial products.

Some evidence also suggests that risks of new market entry are higher than risks of new product launches.[26] Certainly, it is ill advised to enter new foreign markets without some basic marketing research to assess those markets, and yet such research is often not commissioned until after the initial attempts to enter have failed. Consideration of the growth strategies of multinationals sheds some insight into these problems. Figure 1 shows that we can depict the "business" of any modern diversified company by the portfolio of product/market entries of which it consists. Companies can follow a variety of growth vectors to expand their business. Many retailers and some manufacturers — AMF, for example — develop a broader mix of products focused on helping to better meet the needs of a particular market. Such companies, we may say, are "market dominated" in their growth pattern, and they grow by seeking new products and broadening the product line. The horizontal arrow in Figure 1 illustrates this pattern.

Most multinational companies have pursued a primary growth different from to the one just described. The traditional pattern for most has been to take a product or group of products and girdle

---

[26]John Kitching, "Why Do Mergers Miscarry?"*Harvard Business Review*, Vol. 45 (November–December 1967), p. 91.

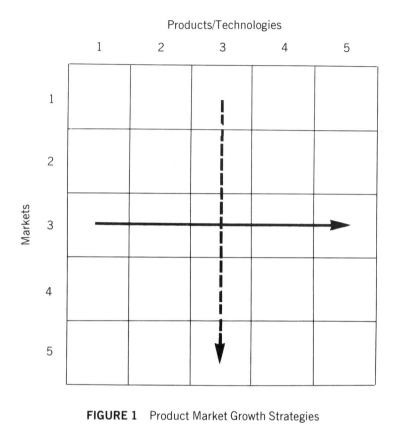

FIGURE 1 Product Market Growth Strategies

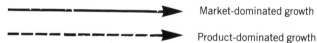

the globe with them, seeking all new markets. When these growth opportunities are exhausted, the company begins to look elsewhere — that is, to new technologies and products — for growth. The growth histories of international companies such as Gillette, Singer, Coats-Patons, and Honda confirm this interpretation, and have followed the vertical arrow in Figure 1. Such a growth orientation, labeled "product dominated," is the most common among manufacturers.

Several implications arise from this observation. The perceived strength of companies, as inferred from their expansion vectors, lies in their product, technological, or manufacturing expertise. Yet, to grow they must seek and develop new markets. To profit from their products — and to amortize the ever-increasing capital costs of their innovations — demands an ability to develop new markets. Also implied is a considerable shift in orientation, from manufacturing or research and development to marketing. This change must coincide with a shift from a domestic outlook to a global perspective. The transition, we believe, has been successfully accomplished by few companies, and this accounts for some of the misdirected marketing effort observed in international markets.

The above conclusions are based not only on our survey but also on our personal experience in working with multinationals and on other attempts to analyze corporate strategies.[27] The findings are consistent with this interpretation, especially when placed in the context of our discussion of control in Chapter 6. For example, if market research and market information are crucial to reduction of market risk in new product introduction, we should expect to find such a department or function established very early in the life of a new subsidiary, even if its work was involved in coordinating outside suppliers. Yet, only about half the subsidiaries with sales of less than $50 million had market research departments, compared with over 80 percent of the larger subsidiaries. As so often occurs, companies manage costs and problems closer than revenues and opportunities, particularly if their orientation is internal. This is quite common, particularly in American companies; we explore the issue again later in the book.

SUMMARY

In this chapter we have examined the issues of subsidiary strategy and performance. Although interwoven with approaches to planning and control, we have focused on the formulation of objectives and strategies, the role of the home office in this process, and the performance results. We have argued that objectives and strategies of the subsidiary should reflect its stage of development and its organizational structure and resources, and by and large this is what we found. We also observed a lack of correspondence between control criteria and performance objectives — a prelude to

[27]Ansoff, *op. cit.*
J. P. Sallenave, *La Strategie de l'Entreprise Face à la Concurrence* (Paris: Les Editions d'Organisation, 1973).

Chapter 6 — which suggests some serious problems. We examined some of the issues involved in attempting to measure subsidiary performance. For our Brazilian sample at least, there is little reason to suspect wholesale reporting bias, and on this basis profitability of multinational subsidiaries and of their Brazilian domestic counterparts was roughly similar. Finally, we reviewed some of the broader issues involved in program standardization and growth strategy, concluding that zeal for the former may sometimes be driven by the overall company orientation.

Chapter **5**

Managing the Communications Flow

Communications is the lifeblood of the modern multinational enterprise. The technical, managerial, and market expertise that flows through the many channels created by the organization structure is an important contributor to the competitive edge of the multinational firm. Without the explosive postwar changes in communications and transportation, the interdependent fiefdoms of the multinational corporation would be inconceivable.

Managing the communications flow, however, represents a chronic headache from which few firms have found relief. The same questions arise: What types of information should be sent? How much of it is necessary? How often should it be sent? Too much communication overwhelms headquarters and subsidiary alike; too little limits effective decision making. Likewise, incorrect or merely inappropriate information can disrupt operations as easily as a dearth of information.

Communications serve several important roles for the multinational firm. The most obvious function is the transfer of information from one part of the company to another, either from the parent to its foreign subsidiaries or vice versa. From the parent flows information on such subjects as new product research and development, marketing programs for new and standard products, accounting systems, and other matters. For their part, subsidiaries are feeding back information on their performance, local market conditions, competitive developments, and other facts relevant to their local market area.

Helping to coordinate and integrate the diverse elements of the multinational firm is another critical role of communications. The geographical, cultural, language, and market differences subsumed by a multinational firm compound the already difficult coordination task. To achieve some unity of effort for the firm as a whole requires a considerable amount of integration.[1] Integration relies heavily on communications flow between subunits, and in the multinational company, flows between headquarters and the foreign subsidiary are critical.

As the multinational firm has evolved, integration has become increasingly important. First, the increase in the cross supplying of raw materials, components, and finished products between subsidiaries at home and abroad demands a well-integrated framework of operations. Second, communication helps to foster mutual understanding among managers with very diverse backgrounds, perspectives, and responsibilities.[2]

The controls exercised by headquarters over foreign affiliates are also critically dependent on rapid and efficient communication flows. Communication is the means through which headquarters signals problems, guides strategic decisions, feeds the planning process, and measures performance of the subsidiary. As we observe below, the sophistication of controls in the modern multinational firm has dramatically expanded the flow of communications used for this purpose.

Even though computers, satellites, and jet airplanes have facilitated the rapid growth of communication capabilities, other problems have arisen as a result. By making communication easier, these innovations have increased the tendency for waste and misdirection, with insufficient concern about the time and cost required to prepare and utilize the additional information. In many firms quantity of information flow has taken priority over its quality and potential utility. Indeed, Chorafas found that few managers

[1]Paul R. Lawrence and Jay W. Lorsch, *Organization and Environment: Managing Differentiation & Integration* (Boston: Division of Research, Graduate School of Business Administration, Harvard University, 1967).
[2]Wickham Skinner, *American Industry in Developing Economies* (New York: John Wiley & Sons, 1968), p. 177.

were sensitive to the true costs of communication in terms of time, effort, and direct expenses.[3]

Thus, although the control role of communications is evident, continuing problems arise over the volume and purpose of the communications flow. Difficulties also arise from discrepancies in background and knowledge about local conditions, as well as such factors as diversity of native language and cultural antecedents. In the following sections we look first at the types of communication flowing between home offices and subsidiaries; then at some of the factors affecting how much and how often different kinds of communication occurred. Next, we note some of the consequences of communications and areas where information needs are not adequately met. Finally, we present some suggestions for better management of communication systems.

COMMUNICATING WITH THE FOREIGN SUBSIDIARY

Our survey of foreign subsidiaries in Brazil considered several dimensions of the communications system between headquarters and subsidiary, including:

- Type of information flows.
- Characteristics and conditions affecting the flows.
- Benefits and problems resulting from the communications.

Communications can be classified in a number of ways, each with its own advantages and limitations. We chose to separate communications into two broad categories: (1) impersonal flows such as the reporting system, budgets, plans, telexes, and letters and (2) personal communication in the form of visits, company meetings, and telephone conversations. To limit the scope we focused primarily on the flows between the subsidiary chief executive or marketing manager and his superior at headquarters.

Impersonal Communication

Regular Reports to Headquarters.   Much of the information from the subsidiary to headquarters was reported on a standard-

[3]Dimitris N. Chorafas, *The Communication Barrier in International Management* (New York: American Management Association, Research Study No. 100, 1969), p. 17.

ized form either weekly, monthly, quarterly, or annually. These reports included statements of profit and loss, balance sheet positions, sales, sources and uses of funds, deposits and loans, exposed assets, inventory positions, production schedules and output, production and marketing costs, and deviations from budget expectations.

Market and sales results were sent home monthly, or even more often, by every company surveyed. These reports ranged from a simple statement of total sales volume to a detailed breakdown by product, market segment, selling price, market share, and expenses. Several American subsidiaries reported weekly or every ten days. In most companies the chief executive reported to the home office sales and marketing results as part of the summary statement or package of reports. However, in one out of every three companies, the marketing manager reported the information directly to the home office.

Financial and production statements were forwarded to the home office on a monthly basis by over 80 percent of the companies. European companies tended to report financial results less frequently.

Many other reports were forwarded regularly and in various degrees of detail. Among American companies a favorite was the chief executive letter, a three- to five-page summary of activities inside and outside the company, designed to give the home office an overview and explanation of the numerical results.

Home Office Response.   What becomes of the subsidiary report when it arrives at headquarters? Does it receive careful evaluation and thoughtful response, or is it "filed for future reference"? Most subsidiary managers believe that the majority of their reports are read and evaluated by headquarters staff. In Japanese companies, headquarters personnel confirmed that this was so. Firms with *more* overseas subsidiaries seem to do a better job of evaluating reports than those with fewer subsidiaries. In firms with more foreign subsidiaries the home office often responds by adding to its staff persons who are responsible for reading and evaluating the greater number of reports. As might be expected, well-established subsidiaries receive somewhat less attention from headquarters in these matters. There was no indication, however, that the nationality of the company affects the evaluation process.

Some home offices reply to subsidiary reports on a regular basis; many others follow a management-by-exception policy — becoming involved only when they spot a problem or an opportunity. Among the American firms, nearly one-half respond each month according to a fixed schedule (for example, reports received at the home office on the third day of the month are answered by the tenth). Such a pattern of scheduled responses was found in less than 10 percent of European and Japanese home offices, where it was common practice to respond only when necessary. In fact, in some of these companies the practice has perhaps gone too far: 20 percent of the chief executives claimed that they rarely or never receive a reply to a report.

Subsidiary executives criticized both extremes. Managers of American subsidiaries generally felt that home office comments were "incisive" and "useful" but complained that "they (home office staff) spend too much time circling budget variances and asking why." One European derided home office personnel as "those superspecialized specialists who only see one tree in the forest. As a result, all they do is give us trouble." Timeliness of responses is another criticism. Home office comments are often elaborate but come too late to be useful. One manager commented: "We get this beautiful computer printout showing us where we stand and what to do, but the February results arrive on May 1. By this time we've already corrected our mistakes or we're in big trouble."

In contrast, some managers of European and Japanese companies wished they received more support from the home office. "They send us out here and then forget us back home" is the complaint of these executives, who sometimes felt that their corporation was passing them by. These attitudes reflect more than communication factors, since they may also relate to the company's treatment of its overseas managers in general, including its procedures for their selection, rotation, and promotion.

Reports from Headquarters. The actual number of reports, brochures, and manuals sent from the home office to Brazil was difficult to measure precisely, but our estimate indicates that American companies sent substantially more materials than did foreign companies to assist and coordinate subsidiary operations. Subsidiaries with several divisions or product lines received somewhat fewer reports — perhaps an indication that where numerous home office divisions were involved, the voluntary flow of information to Brazil was reduced. On the other hand, it could also be that multidivision subsidiaries tend to be more self-sufficient, thereby requesting less information from the home office.

Although we did not directly measure the flow of telexes and letters for purposes other than reporting, we observed that the chief executives of American subsidiaries relied more heavily on the telex and telephone than their European counterparts. American managers frequently commented that "when I want an answer I phone the boss in New York." Frequently such calls were to "touch base," as Americans call it, or to see whether home office concurs or, more accurately, whether it does not disagree with a decision well within the authority of the local manager. In marked contrast to Americans, many chief executives of European subsidiaries were proud of the fact that they seldom called headquarters. In some Japanese companies, where decisions were still made largely in Tokyo, proposals were telexed from Brazil in the evening and the decision was received by the next morning. The twelve-hour time difference gave headquarters an entire working day to make the decision.

Effect of Culture.   We have already alluded to some of the differences in reporting practice among multinational firms of different national origins. Considering the total flow of impersonal communications, American subsidiaries had far heavier reporting requirements than their Japanese or European counterparts. In fact, the effect of nationality on reporting procedures was much stronger than any other characteristic of headquarters or the subsidiary.[4]

Considering their heavy reporting burden, it was not surprising that managers in American firms complained most bitterly about "all those damn reports." Marketing managers in American companies estimated that they devoted 20 percent of their time to collecting, collating, and interpreting information requested by the home office. This means that, on average, they spent one day a week "keeping the home office happy." In contrast, their counterparts in European companies spent 10 percent of their time on such duties, and in Japanese firms, only 8 percent.

[4]Characteristics which explained little or no differences in impersonal communications included the level of worldwide and subsidiary sales as a percent of world sales, and length of time established in Brazil.

Chief executives of American subsidiaries also spent more time on reporting functions. Because many of them began their careers at a time when written reports were the exception rather than the rule, the thought of reports often caused real frustration. One manager complained: "These reporting forms are so complicated, I'm the only person who understands them down here. This means I spend two or three days every month filling out these reams of paper just to keep people in New York off my back." Other Americans voiced similar criticism, in one case referring to headquarters as the "paper mill." In fairness, it is worth noting that "report-writing blues" were not a unique trait of American managers; several European and Japanese executives were equally frustrated by the heavy burden of reports.

Personal Communication

Visits to and from Headquarters. Personal interaction is a principal source of information for executives in domestic and foreign business alike.[5] Perhaps as a backlash to the barrage of documents and reports, many managers indicate that "there's no substitute for personal contact." Executives at headquarters and in Brazil claimed that no matter how sophisticated the flow of impersonal communication, personal contact was by far their most important source of knowledge.

The managers in the survey spent a good deal of time meeting with home office personnel. Again, American companies were the most devoted to the "personal-visits syndrome." Table 1 illustrates that managers of American companies visited their home office an average of 2.2 times a year. This compares with 1.5 visits for the Europeans and 1.6 for the Japanese.

---

[5]Keegan observed that 67 percent of all important external information was obtained through human sources. See Warren J. Keegan, "Multinational Scanning: A Study of the Information Sources Utilized by Headquarters Executives in Multinational Companies," *Administrative Science Quarterly*, Vol. 19, (1974), pp. 411–422. Similar results were reported by F. J. Aguilar, *Scanning the Business Environment*, (London: Macmillan, 1967), p. 94; and T. J. Allen, "The Differential Performance of Information Channels in the Transfer of Technology" in W. H. Gruber and D. G. Marquis (eds.), *Factors in the Transfer of Technology* (Cambridge, Mass: M.I.T. Press, 1969), pp. 137–154.

Table 1

Personal Visits between Subsidiary and Home Office

Nationality of Parent Company	A. Visits between Chief Executive in Brazil and Home Office Superiors — Median Visits a Year			
	To Home Office by Chief Executive	To Brazil by Home Office Superiors	Total Visits	Number of Companies
American	2.2	2.7	4.9	24
European	1.5	1.1	2.6	28
Japanese	1.6	1.1	2.7	11
	1.8	1.4	3.2	63

Nationality of Parent Company	B. Visits between Marketing Manager in Brazil and Home Office Superiors — Median Visits a Year			
	To Home Office by Marketing Manager	To Brazil by Home Office Superiors	Total Visits	Number of Companies
American	1.5	5.6	7.1	29
European	0.7	1.3	2.2	25
Japanese	0.3	1.5	1.5	8
	0.9	2.3	3.4	62

The same pattern holds for trips to the subsidiary by superiors from headquarters. On average, American subsidiaries were visited twice as often as were other firms by executives directly responsible for the subsidiary in Brazil. Thus, in total, executives of American subsidiaries met face to face with their bosses 4.8 times a year, or roughly every eleven weeks. In contrast, visits in European firms were exchanged a total of 2.6 times a year and 2.7 times in Japanese companies.

For second-level managers the differences were even more pronounced. Marketing managers of American companies visited the home office more frequently and in turn received many more visits from home office people providing marketing assistance.

Influences on Visitation Patterns. Why do we find such notable differences in visitation practices from company to company? What are the effects of such visits? Besides the differences attributable to national origin, one factor stands out — the number of visits is directly associated with the size and complexity of the parent company. As firms grow and establish more overseas subsidiaries, visits to and from headquarters become more frequent.

Economies of scale operate in favor of larger companies, making it more efficient and economical to visit several subsidiaries on one overseas trip. Furthermore, as noted in Chapter 2, some larger corporations have elaborate and multilayered organizational structures, the effect of which is that impersonal communication is sometimes filtered and delayed. Personal visits can, of course, break these bottlenecks and facilitate the information flow with less misunderstanding.

Size alone is not the only influence on personal visits, nor does it explain why American firms rely on them so heavily. Some have suggested, for example, that because Brazil is so important to American multinational corporations, headquarters watches it more closely. Yet we observed (Table 1, Appendix D) that Brazilian sales as a percent of world sales were higher on average for the Europeans (3.6 percent) than for the Americans (2.1 percent). This being true, we should expect closer scrutiny from European home offices. Furthermore, the number of fatiguing time-zone changes between Brazil and European headquarters (four hours) is not drastically different from the number between Brazil and American headquarters (one to four hours). It is our conclusion, to be developed further in Chapter 6, that the intensive visitation patterns are part of an extensive and formal control system adopted by many American companies.

The number of personal visits, however, should not be considered synonymous with effective communication. Successful personal visits require preparation and planning at each level of the organization; yet rarely is either done sufficiently well, and the visits accomplish little. Because key personnel or relevant information is unavailable, decisions must be postponed. On other occasions the home office executive is making a "whistle stop" tour of Latin America or Europe, which, after his visit to the second or third country, becomes rather ineffectual. Such brief stopovers also make it easier for subsidiary managers to avoid, or hide from the executive, problem areas within the subsidiary.

Although a few European executives in our survey wished to see their home office superiors more often, many European and American managers suffered from overexposure to headquarters. "We've been discovered," complained one in Rio; "every year between December and March, when it's cold in New York, we're overrun with visitors." One subsidiary, which in one year played host to nearly four hundred "official" visitors from the home office, now requires that such visits be approved beforehand by the subsidiary's manager. Other subsidiaries are following this practice to reduce "vacation" visits; some even require a visit evaluation before the visitor leaves the country. This criticism is not meant to denigrate the value of purposeful face-to-face conversation between home office and subsidiary managers. The concern is that visits sometimes become perfunctory, made because "it's time we see what's going on in Brazil," not for any pressing need. Managers at both levels agree that they gain something from such visits, but at what cost in terms of managerial time, energy, and direct expenses? In many firms, especially those with a dearth of effective international managers, the opportunity costs of unnecessary personal visits can be enormous.

Company Meetings. Besides personal visits, over half the companies interviewed held regular meetings during which subsidiary managers confer with regional or home office personnel for two or three days. The rationale behind such meetings is simple. They offer opportunities through lectures and workshops to communicate company goals and strategies, to unveil new products and technology, and to interact with managers from headquarters, sister subsidiaries, and sometimes product divisions. In some companies these meetings were held for a region or an area; in others for product divisions; in still others for subsidiary managers around the world.

In our survey American firms held these management conferences with far greater frequency than either the Europeans or the Japanese. Most manager meetings included the chief executives from all worldwide subsidiaries, although a number of American companies were moving to both worldwide and regional meetings on an annual basis. The number of foreign subsidiaries in the global network was also an important influence on whether companies held such meetings. As the network grows, the company conference becomes an efficient means of communicating corporate goals, strategies, and programs for the coming year.

Nearly two-thirds of the American parent companies also held meetings specifically for their marketing managers, a practice far less common in European and Japanese companies. Several non-American managers criticized the practice of regular meetings.

One Japanese saltily reported: "No, we don't have any jamborees . . . we used to, but found them a waste of time." Another hard-bitten European chided the Americans for their "annual world Christmas parties."

Certain industries, such as pharmaceuticals and domestic appliances, tended to hold more regional marketing meetings. For these products, headquarters was closely involved in the marketing programs and apparently found it efficient and effective to call a meeting to present the annual program.

BUILDING A COMMUNICATIONS SYSTEM

The preceding discussion has evaluated each type of communications flow on an individual basis. An important issue arising from this analysis is the extent to which firms have constructed a formalized system for multiple communication flows. Do the firms that rely on personal visits and management conferences also maintain an extensive reporting system, or do personal and impersonal communications substitute for one another?

The correlation coefficients in Table 2 answer three questions about the relationships between different communication flows. In the upper triangle, labeled A, the correlation coefficients indicate that different types of impersonal communication generally complemented one another. Firms submitting more reports to headquarters typically received more reports in return. Although the correlations are not significant in some cases, they suggest that some firms had at least developed elaborate systems for reporting up and down the hierarchy, and that these systems were complete with staff groups to evaluate and respond to subsidiary problems and opportunities.

For personal communication, the results indicate positive but generally weak relationships between visits to and from headquarters and corporate meetings (see triangle B in Table 2). Since personal visits, except for planning reviews, are likely to occur more on an "as needed" basis, the low correlations in this instance are not surprising. Looking at the two classes of communication together (triangle C in Table 2), we observe that personal and impersonal communications generally operated as complements rather than substitutes. Van de Ven and his coworkers found sub-

Table 2
Simple Correlations between Personal and Impersonal Communication between Headquarters and Foreign Subsidiary[a] (N = 63)

	1	2	3	4	5	6	7
1 Reports to headquarters	—						
2 Reports from headquarters	.16†	—					
3 Headquarters evaluation of reports	.11	−.13					
4 Frequency of headquarter's response	.23‡	.01	.40‡	—			
5 Visits to headquarters	.14*	−.04	.01	.15*	—		
6 Visits from headquarters	.23†	−.05	.32‡	.34‡	.08	—	
7 Corporate meeting	.07	.02	.01	.05	.06	.09	—

[a]*Kendall Tau correlation coefficients*
* p < .10   † p < .05   ‡ p < .01

stitutions of different forms of communication.[6] Without an evaluation of the relative importance of each mode, however, our research suggests that conditions requiring greater coordination result in the use of both written reports and face-to-face meeting in an additive manner.

The generally weak intramodal relationships observed in triangles A and B suggested that some other classification system might yield additional insight into patterns of communication and their causes. A factor analysis of the raw data (see Table 1 in Appendix C) resulted in a breakdown by source or origin of the communication rather than by type. Thus, instead of viewing communica-

[6]Andrew H. Van de Ven, Andre L. Delbecq, and Richard Koenig, Jr., "Determinants of Coordination Modes Within Organizations," *American Sociological Review*, Vol. 41 (April 1976), pp. 322–338.

tions as personal or impersonal, this analysis suggested that the underlying explanation of communication patterns rests with the source of the communication, whether it is initiated by headquarters or the foreign subsidiary.

Identifying the factors that determine where communications originate, we observed that the number of foreign subsidiaries was the driving force in increasing communications from home office. (See Table 2 in Appendix C for results of the regression analysis.) Not only do more subsidiaries reduce the per subsidiary cost of personal visits, but headquarters also receives and produces more information on worldwide activities, which can then be communicated to subsidiaries through reports. As the number of subsidiaries increases, so does the complexity of managing international operations and the size of the headquarters staff. Thus, with size, importance, and complexity of international operations all increasing, heavier outflows of communication become an inevitable consequence.

Firms requiring sizable capital investment also initiated more communication from headquarters. In these cases, operating economics are undoubtedly an important influence, since headquarters tends to remain more involved for purposes of coordination and control.[7] Younger subsidiaries also received more communications from the home office — not surprising, in view of the risks faced by new subsidiary operations and their need for the expertise and resources supplied by the parent company.

When the subsidiary was managed by a national executive instead of an expatriate, the volume of headquarters-initiated communication was significantly lower. In our view, this finding supports the conclusion that despite the multinational nomenclature, most firms are far from multinational in practice.[8] Indeed, host-country nationals are often relatively isolated in the global system. We further explore this view later in the chapter.

Two characteristics of the parent company influenced the flow of communications initiated by the subsidiary. Compared with American firms, European and Japanese subsidiaries initiated far fewer communications, even though nationality was not impor-

[7]Skinner, *op. cit.*

[8]Howard V. Perlmutter and David A. Heenan, "How Multinational Should Your Top Managers Be?" *Harvard Business Review,* Vol. 54, No. 6 (November–December 1976), pp. 121–132.

tant in determining the flow of communication from headquarters. Second, a large parent company in terms of worldwide sales encouraged a much heavier flow of communication from subsidiaries than did a smaller parent. As observed earlier, greater size generally leads to more formalized and standardized formats, procedures, and staff groups. The inexorable result is to encourage greater flows of information from the outlying subsidiaries to the home office.

THE EFFECTS OF COMMUNICATION

Does the Home Office Understand?

How do reports, visits, conferences, and other forms of communication influence the working relationships between the home office and the subsidiary managers? Does communication enhance understanding, or does the burden of reports and meetings lead to frustration and dissension? Our survey included a question that asked subsidiary executives how well they thought headquarters understood their problems. Nearly half believed that home office superiors and staff did not comprehend the problems in Brazil.

What kinds of companies were noted for better or worse understanding?[9] Managers of Japanese companies felt that their home office had a poor understanding of what was going on in their subsidiaries. Indeed, several claimed that relations with headquarters posed bigger problems than relations with the Brazilian government or personnel problems within the subsidiary.[10] Considering that many of the Japanese companies had entered Brazil rather recently, this finding is not surprising. When it comes to overseas manufacturing, most Japanese multinationals were newcomers compared to their European and American competitors.

---

[9]A more thorough evaluation of this question is presented in Table 3 of Appendix C.

[10]It is interesting to note the results when home office managers of Japanese companies who were responsible for Brazilian operations were asked this question in reverse form. From their viewpoint, in Japan they recognized limitations in their understanding to be greater than these limitations were perceived to be by their own subsidiary managers in Brazil.

"We are still learning," claimed one executive. "Twenty-five years ago we knew very little about exporting, and we learned. Now we have to learn how to manufacture outside of Japan and Southeast Asia." The sharp cultural differences between Japan and Brazil make the transition more difficult, but Japanese subsidiaries with a longer tenure in the country have solved these problems reasonably well. One manager warned, however, that the contrasting time perspectives of the Japanese and Brazilians may lead to serious frustrations, particularly in joint-venture operations. "It's like sitting at opposite ends of a table. The Brazilians are in a hurry; they want profits now. We're in less of a hurry; we're willing to take our time with profits."

Besides the Japanese influence on home office understanding, we also found that companies with high capital intensity enjoyed better understanding. Decisions to invest large amounts of capital demand extensive planning and monitoring, all of which tend to enhance home office comprehension of the overseas situation.

One might expect that companies which are more active in international operations would also display better understanding of subsidiary problems. The results do not support this hypothesis. Neither the parent company's size nor its proportion of overseas sales was associated with how well the home office was thought to understand the subsidiary's situation in Brazil. The subsidiary's sales volume also had no effect on understanding, but product-line complexity was important. Executives of more diversified firms perceived less understanding at the home office. As more people (divisions) become involved at the home office in providing technical and product support, the likelihood of confusion, bottlenecks, and misunderstandings also appears to increase.

The flow of communications — number of reports, personal visits, or conferences — had no substantial effect on perceived levels of understanding. What is done with reports did seem important, however. If the subsidiary manager believed that his reports were being carefully read and evaluated, he also felt that the home office better understood his problems.

In the opinion of many managers, the downward flow of reports from headquarters to subsidiary only reduced understanding. Whether this reflected real misunderstanding by the home office or the manager's backlash reaction against the barrage of reports from headquarters was not apparent. What is clear, however, is that increasing the quality and relevancy rather than quantity of information flow is most important.

Desire for More Information

Although no one volunteered to send more information *to* the home office, one of every three executives wanted more help *from* headquarters. Some desired very specific information.

- What is going on in world markets?
- How will regional or worldwide economic and political conditions affect our markets?
- What is happening to sister subsidiaries who might be manufacturing and selling similar products?
- What marketing strategies have succeeded or failed elsewhere?
- What technical problems might be encountered with a new product or process?

Others simply desired to participate more actively in the corporate family circle, to feel less isolated from sister subsidiaries and the parent company. Some European subsidiary executives claimed that they learned more from home country bank representatives than from headquarters. Regardless of details, most executives sought a better quality of information rather than greater quantity. Illustrating this dilemma, one manager quipped, "I've already taken two speed-reading courses to keep up with all these reports. What I really need is some way to wade through the ninety percent of irrelevancies and spot the ten percent that's useful."

Despite some company-by-company differences, a number of generalizations are important.[11] Firms requiring a lower capital intensity — for example, food or pharmaceutical manufacturers, which tended to enjoy lower levels of home office understanding — were the most eager for additional information from the home office.

Companies headed by national executives also desired more support from headquarters. These managers were generally less familiar with home office policies and politics and were therefore forced to rely on "proper channels" to acquire the desired information. Since these channels were often filtered or blocked, the

[11]The reader is referred to Table 4 of Appendix C for more details.

manager became frustrated in his quest for help. As companies hire more nationals for top-management positions, the seriousness of this problem is likely to grow. As we observed earlier, subsidiaries run by national managers reportedly received fewer communications initiated by headquarters. Thus, their desire for more information seems entirely reasonable.

Among the companies not desiring more information were those receiving regular feedback from the home office. This may reflect an *après le déluge* response; as one manager commented: "Home office doesn't always send the help we need, but we certainly don't want any more reports or guidelines; we can't read what we receive now." Others also noted that when headquarters responds to every detail — a practice labeled "variance circling" by some executives — the feeling of being scrutinized can elicit resentment toward any form of home office "intrusion," whether or not it is helpful. Thus, sometimes excessive feedback can lead to a backlash against any type of information from headquarters, even though the subsidiary might in fact need assistance.

IMPROVING THE COMMUNICATIONS SYSTEM

The findings reported up to this point have described some of the components of communication systems used by a cross section of multinational firms. From a manager's viewpoint the question remains — how can the system be used more effectively?

An answer to this question implies that a criterion is available by which to measure the effectiveness of communications. In our survey better understanding between headquarters and the subsidiary was used. Although this may well encourage smoother working relationships, it represents only one aspect of effective communications.

A broader criterion seeks to measure the impact of communication on the attainment of subsidiary and parent company objectives. Evaluating such direct effects is often difficult, however, and we are forced to rely on less comprehensive measures, such as those used in the survey.

Using these measures, we uncovered a number of problems and concerns about the communication systems currently employed. The following discussion provides a checklist of considerations designed to improve the flow of information in the multi-national firm.

Planning Communications

Few companies bother to assess systematically the costs and benefits of intrafirm communication. Even if attempted, most analyses would focus on direct or out-of-pocket costs. Yet in many firms these costs are minor compared with the less visible opportunity costs. The costs of misdirected or untimely communications, the costs in managerial time diverted from more fruitful endeavors — these are the true costs of poorly managed communications.

The term "managed communications" does not simply imply that communication should be more systematic. Companies using standardized reporting formats often end up drowning in their own paperwork. Managing communications requires a continuous review of the necessity for various reports, meetings, and visits. It means being selective in requesting and distributing documents and in calling meetings. It means making sure that communications do not occur as a form of ritual, but are responsive to problems and opportunities. It may also require a specific individual, an information czar, with the authority to ensure that the system is in fact managed.

A planned communications system is one which evolves over time, in response to strategic and structural changes in the company. Although our survey covered subsidiaries in only one host country at one point in time, we noted considerable differences in communication practices, depending upon such factors as the total number of foreign subsidiaries, maturity of the subsidiary, and capital intensity and size of the firm. As the parent company evolves over the years, it is essential to modify the communications system. Firms with fewer subsidiaries can survive reasonably well without standardized reports and procedures. Such lack of standardization becomes increasingly difficult, however, as the number of subsidiaries and company sales grows. Similarly, as subsidiaries move from their early days as suckling infants to become thriving adolescents or young adults, communications to and from headquarters should be altered to meet changing needs and conditions. Planning communications, therefore, is a dynamic process, not a static, one-time event.

Directing Communications

The direction of communications is associated with its role in the planning process. Within that context, we have chosen to focus on the dual problems of selectivity and responsiveness. From the survey it was clear that many companies were searching actively for a system which could improve the timeliness and accuracy of information flow. The prevailing attitude in many American companies is that more is better: when in doubt send all the information. Following this rule burdens the reader of the information with the problem of sifting and sorting to find the useful data and does little to improve understanding between the home office and the subsidiary. In contrast, the thinking in some European companies is quite the opposite: send nothing unless it is requested and even then do not be in a hurry about sending it. Such a practice wastes time, creates frustration, and leads to decisions based on limited information.

Relevancy as well as quality of information is the key criterion often ignored in the standardized reporting systems of many firms. Under pressure to fill the blanks on the reporting form, the person filling out the form is less concerned with providing accurate data and more concerned with completing the form. Although in some cases numerical guesstimates may be better than no information, our survey suggested that such exercises occur far more often than they should. Consequently, effective planning and decision making become a charade. Improved selectivity would therefore not only reduce the burden of needless communications; it should also help improve the quality of the information used.

Being selective also requires tailoring the communications system to meet the needs of its users, and directing the flow of paperwork and personal interactions to the appropriate individuals in a timely way. These directives are not new to executives with a background in marketing, but as several executives noted, to channel the communication flows and to market ideas within their own companies are often more difficult than marketing to their customers.

Implementing changes, however, requires more than a standardized format. Just as there are "segments" in the customer market, so are there "segments" among executives within the firm. These segments differ in their need for information, and the system should be sensitive to those needs. Perhaps the clearest example is provided by the chief executives in our study, who were native Brazilians. Their reported sense of isolation suggests that they need special consideration and responsiveness from the home offices.

Organizing the Communications Effort

As multinational companies expand their international activities, the need for information and coordination causes a severe strain on traditional organizational structures. The heavy flows of product, functional, and geographical information create bottlenecks in the formal structure, which soon lead to informal and often haphazard channels. Such jerry-built systems may solve the immediate problem, but the long-run costs in time and effectiveness may be considerable.

As we noted in Chapter 2, the evolution of multinational operations creates the need for new forms of organizational structure. The area of managing home office/subsidiary communications systems provides examples of the kinds of stresses that can develop, which lead to suggestions for some necessary modifications. For example, communication flows may be coordinated through a special international information center responsible for collecting, collating, interpreting, and disseminating information requests and flows in both directions. This center could work at the regional or headquarters level, but it must have sufficient authority to request or purchase needed information support from product divisions or staff groups.

Another way of improving coordination for larger firms might be to establish a "desk officer" system similar to the U.S. State Department. These officers should have working knowledge and experience with particular subsidiaries and would be responsible in some manner for coordinating the affairs between the home office and the subsidiaries. The extent of their involvement would depend largely on the size and the needs of the subsidiaries.

In either case it seems clear that the well-structured organization charts and reporting relationships so common in American companies will eventually give way to a new organizational form. Multiple and freer flowing relationships will probably become more common. Organizations will be set up to enhance the flow of information and reports across and through the classic formal structure. Dotted-line relationships between managers who formally have different bosses will be one means of facilitating this flow.

Controlling the Communications Program

Implied in the foregoing discussion is a need to continuously monitor the communications system. As the company itself grows and changes, so must its communications system. All too often, however, the growth of communications far outstrips that of the company itself. Consider, for example, the experience of Marks and Spencer, a well-known and successful British retailer.[12] During the late 1950s, the company was able to eliminate no fewer than 26 million forms used annually, and to reduce its staff progressively from 27,000 to 20,000. By the early 1970s, however, "fast-rising administrative expenses and ever-increasing demands for more staff," recognized as "the familiar signs of trouble," began to recur. Formation of a senior executive task force with a mandate to "get out into the business" and "look afresh at the operations of the company" worked with such effectiveness that millions of reports were eliminated and staff was reduced from 27,000 to 26,000 by 1974, this time without the benefits of the computer solution, which had undoubtedly helped in the 1950s.

The point is that, left alone, report forms, procedures, and meetings tend to proliferate. Management's task is to plan for both contraception and euthanasia. The task is an important one for maintaining an efficient and effective organization; yet because it should be everybody's job, it often belongs to no one. In the smaller organization, characterized by frequent informal face-to-face communications, monitoring the communications system may be a trivial or an unimportant task. In the multinational firm it is crucial — because it is this flow of communication that enables the company to function.

One means to ensure that a communications system evolves sensibly and systematically is to introduce a communications audit system. The increased speed and reduced cost of transmitting information has led many firms into the trap of "when in doubt, send everything." Few companies have bothered to evaluate the real costs or benefits of such a policy. Our study indicates that sheer volume of information does not necessarily lead to better understanding or better decisions at either end of the pipeline.

The apparent need for additional information by many subsidiaries suggests that home offices may not be doing enough to serve

---

[12]Derek G. Rayner, "A Battle Won in the War on the Paper Bureaucracy," *Harvard Business Review*, Vol. 53, No. 2 (March–April 1975), pp. 8–14.

the subsidiary needs in particular areas. In this case a routine audit of local and home office managers to assess the communications system and possible information needs might spotlight a weakness before it becomes a major problem. The desirability of such an audit will grow as more firms replace expatriate managers with nationals who are less familiar with the home office bureaucracy and system for getting things done.

Indeed, managers at all levels must take the time to consider what information both parties need, how often it should be reported, how specific the data need to be, and who should be responsible for collecting and interpreting the information. We recognize that a multinational corporation operating in sixty nations cannot develop a unique system for each market, but within a standardized system some adjustments and deviations can be tolerated.

Furthermore, too often a random request for specific data in one market gets locked into the worldwide reporting system, never to be questioned again as to why it is there or what purpose it serves. A brief anecdote by a high-ranking home office executive illustrates this phenomenon.

Several years ago our company president was asked about the market share for a minor product in Helsinki, Finland. When he learned that no one at home office knew the answer, he demanded that henceforth every overseas subsidiary would report market share figures monthly, broken down by market segments for all products. While this may be a simple exercise in the U.S., it's hardly an easy task in Peru, Thailand, or most of the other forty-plus markets we operate in. Nonetheless we now receive market share data each month — we know it's garbage and the subsidiaries know it too, but we continue to play the game. Please don't ask me how much it probably costs us each year.

Finally, better controls must be established over the flow of communication from home office to subsidiary. On the basis of our survey, the drawbacks of routine responses to monthly subsidiary reports may exceed the benefits. Of course it is important for subsidiary reports to be read and evaluated by headquarters, but a detailed critique of subsidiary performance each month may be excessive. Feedback that highlights potential problems or opportunities is generally well received by local managers. However, repeated reports that simply circle budget variances and request reasons for the variances can create resentment toward any form of help from the home office, even when it might be needed.

These problems are compounded when home office personnel are unfamiliar with the local conditions in which the subsidiary operates. In such situations the home office should be even more careful about the type of information it requests. Frequently, data such as market potential or market share are not readily available for specific products, and the costs in time, effort, and money required to collect the data may far exceed the value. In Brazilian subsidiaries the problem was exacerbated by the critical shortage of competent managers and trained staff.

SUMMARY

This chapter has focused on the role of communications in facilitating understanding and coordination. It has examined communication practices, some of the factors leading to differences in these practices, and the consequences of the practices. Finally, it has highlighted some of the management issues bearing on the design and operation of the communications system.

The findings strongly suggest that communications within the multinational firm are often poorly managed, if indeed they are managed at all. The quantity of written reports has little impact on how well headquarters is perceived to understand the subsidiary, and at the same time excessive requests for information frequently lead to frustration and discontent among subsidiary managers. However, in Chapter 6 we attempt to illustrate that a major function of subsidiary/headquarters communications may have less to do with actual understanding than with management control.

Headquarters Control of Subsidiary Activities

The very term control conveys some unpleasant connotations. It is fair to say that there are no issues more sensitive, difficult, or contentious in relations between a multinational headquarters and its subsidiaries than those arising in the area of control. To some subsidiary managers, control activities are seen, at best, as burdensome and, at worst, as hostile interventions, disruptive and even counterproductive for the subsidiary's business activities. In some cases this may be an accurate viewpoint; however, in general such views are not justified, and very often result from failure to recognize the purposes and benefits of any control system — on the part of both the subsidiary and the home office.

This chapter begins by taking a broad view of controls, to provide a balanced perspective for the discussion that follows. We then examine the controls being used by the firms we studied, the problems which have arisen from their use, and some ways in which they might be modified and improved both to avoid the problems and to become more effective. We also explore the company characteristics influencing control practices, using these characteristics to develop an evolutionary view of the design of effective control structures. Finally, we should note that this chapter also serves an integrating role, because many of the activities discussed in preceding chapters, such as planning, communications, organization, and the formulation of objectives and strategies, play important parts in the overall control process.

CONTROL PROCESSES

From the headquarters' viewpoint, a control system should perform several fundamental functions. As the exclusive or principal shareholder in the foreign subsidiary, headquarters is naturally concerned, from both legal and financial perspectives, that its investment is being appropriately used to generate returns to its stockholders. However, the parent company should also attempt to seek sufficient control to ensure that it can adequately coordinate and integrate its financial, production, and marketing activities on a multinational basis. These first two functions are usually monitored through that part of the control process with which managers are most familiar: the use of a plan or budget. Thus, from a pragmatic perspective, controls are the means by which we attempt to ensure that actual results are those which were established as objectives in the plan.

This last aspect of control is the one which most readily comes to mind, and is certainly the predominant concern of most operating managers, whether in multinational subsidiaries or elsewhere. However, as Newman points out, successful control demands a future orientation.[1] Yet it is precisely this perspective which is so often lacking in companies' control systems.

Newman distinguishes three different types of control:[2]

Steering controls provide a prediction of results and permit corrective action before the operation is completed. These controls guide the trajectory of subsidiary efforts and represent an a priori attempt to ensure that performance will be effective — that is, meets objectives.

Yes/No controls are basically screening devices which in our context will be viewed as requiring headquarters' approval before a decision may be made.

Postaction controls, as the name implies, take effect after the fact — that is, after action is completed and results are compared with a standard or an objective.

[1] William H. Newman, *Constructive Control: Design and Use of Control Systems* (Englewood Cliffs, N.J.: Prentice-Hall, 1975), pp. 4–7.
[2] *Ibid.,* p. 6.

Although all types of control may be necessary:

Steering controls . . . offer the greatest opportunity for constructive effect. The chief purpose of all controls is to bring actual results as close as possible to desired results, and steering controls provide a mechanism for remedial action while the actual results are still being shaped.[3]

Though less broad than Anthony's view,[4] which includes even planning as part of the control system, Newman offers a comprehensive framework for evaluating control processes, and it is his approach which we adopt in this chapter.

SELECTING SUBSIDIARY BUSINESS OBJECTIVES

The most crucial steering controls for multinational subsidiaries should be their business objectives. Choosing the "right" objectives for a subsidiary is not easy, but once these objectives are selected and incorporated in a plan of action, they should guide many of the subsidiaries' subsequent actions. Researchers who have looked into the issues of subsidiary objectives and performance assessment generally agree that multinationals do a poor job in this regard. Specifically, the criteria chosen are often too inflexible, too financially oriented, and short term in their outlook.[5] Furthermore, in recent years management thinking has become increasingly sophisticated in the area of assessment and evaluation of business performance, although little of this thinking seems yet to have permeated the area of subsidiary management.

Developing Appropriate Business Objectives

Within the preceding ten years, it has become more accepted that for purposes of strategic planning, different kinds of business units

---

[3]*Ibid.*, p. 7.
[4]Robert Anthony
[5]See, for example, Sidney M. Robbins and Robert B. Stobaugh, "The Bent Measuring Stick for Foreign Subsidiaries," *Harvard Business Review,* September –October 1975, pp. 80–88; W. K. Brandt and J. M. Hulbert, *A Empresa Multinacional no Brasil: Um Estudo Empirico* (Rio de Janeiro: Zahar Editores, 1977); Jean-Claude Larréché, "The International Product–Market Portfolio," *Proceedings* of the American Marketing Association, 1978, pp. 276–281; W. K. Brandt and J. M. Hulbert, "Formulating Objectives and Evaluating Performance in the Multinational Subsidiary," *Proceedings* of the American Marketing Association, 1978, pp. 282–284.

(product lines or divisions) require different strategic objectives. In turn, these objectives require unique procedures to evaluate the success or failure of chosen strategies. Indeed, the PIMS (profit impact of marketing strategy) project[6] currently aimed at identifying the influences on profits in more than two thousand businesses was originally initiated by General Electric in an attempt to develop criteria for performance evaluation that better matched the characteristics of particular businesses or product lines.[7]

The notion of ensuring congruence between strategic objectives and evaluation criteria has received additional support from the Boston Consulting Group.[8] This group's analysis of a company's product portfolio focuses explicitly on the distinctive financial characteristics of a business or product at different stages of its life cycle.[9] It also emphasizes consistency between how a business or product is managed and the standards by which its performance is evaluated.

Perhaps an example will help to clarify the approach. Let us consider the case of an innovative company that is launching a new product. If the product is an initial success, the market will begin to grow, usually at an increasing rate. In this stage the company should be focusing on ways to expand the market for its product — either by finding new market segments or by building greater market share. New plants or plant additions must be built and markets developed. Both actions require heavy cash expenditures, much of which may not be recoverable during the first or second year of the new business. During this period accounting statements would typically show a loss for the business. In fact, management cannot and should not expect high profits and high returns on investment during this early stage of the product's life. If the company refuses to yield in its profit expectations, the product will probably not be able to establish a strong position in the market. This may not only jeopardize its entry into the market but will almost certainly limit its longer run profitability.[10]

---

[6]Sidney Schoeffler, Robert D. Buzzell, and Donald F. Heany, "Impact of Strategic Planning on Profit Performance," *Harvard Business Review,* March–April 1974, pp. 137–145.

[7]*Ibid.,* p. 139.

[8]*Perspectives on Experience,* Boston Consulting Group, 1968.

[9]*Growth and Financial Strategies,* Boston Consulting Group, undated.

[10]The PIMS project has demonstrated that the level of market share is the most critical determinant of a product's profitability. See Robert D. Buzzell, Bradley T. Gale, and Ralph G. M. Sultan, "Market Share — a Key to Profitability," *Harvard Business Review,* January–February 1975, pp. 97–106.

Later in the product's life cycle, growth rates begin to slow and profit margins on a per unit basis are typically higher. At this point, the emphasis in strategic objectives should begin to shift away from sales growth in favor of profits.

Finally, as the market matures, competitive pressures on prices often lead to lower profit margins per unit, a reduction that may be offset by high unit sales volumes. At this stage, the strategic objectives should focus more on the generating of cash; incremental investments in the business or product should be carefully scrutinized to ensure that any investments will benefit and not impair the cash-generating capability of the business. Table 1 shows the empirical results for this evolution of financial position among the products making up the PIMS data base.

Though the analogy is not perfect, this framework provides a way of thinking about the evaluation of the performance of multinational subsidiaries. Early in the life of a foreign subsidiary or a new division in a subsidiary, corporate profitability standards simply cannot be achieved without stifling future growth potential. Indeed, in fast-growing markets that characterize many developing countries, rigid demands for profits today might be particularly unwise; some willingness to forgo short-run profits may well enhance future profitability.

As we shall see, however, there is little indication that the concepts discussed above are understood or executed by managers

Table 1
Selected Operating Results of PIMS Businesses by Stage in Product Life Cycle

		Stage in Life Cycle		
Measure	Start-up*	Growth	Early Maturity	Late Maturity
Return on investment	−19	22	22	18
Net income growth	7	20	15	11
Investment growth	38	16	9	6
Cash flow/investment	−46	−2	4	4
Marketing/sales	26	10	10	8

Data are four-year average percentages, except growth rates, which are annual rates in current dollars, and data in the start-up column, which are medians.

SOURCE: *Pimsletter,* "The Senior Executive Tight-Wire Act: Balancing the Portfolio of Businesses," No. 10, Cambridge, Mass.: The Strategic Planning Institute, 1978, p. 5.

at multinational company headquarters. In most firms, upper level home office managers continue to focus on the short run and do not generally accept the view that their overseas ventures represent a portfolio of businesses that need to be managed and evaluated in different ways.

Criteria Used for Performance Evaluation

It would seem unreasonable if some consistent relationship did not exist between business objectives and the standards used to evaluate subsidiary performance. If there is no congruence, then the steering controls and the postaction controls may be operating at cross purposes. In fact, although limited empirical evidence is available on the subject, on balance it suggests that there is indeed a conflict built into the control systems of many companies.

The most ambitious study directed at this issue was conducted by the Conference Board.[11] A survey of the home offices of 115 U.S. companies revealed that conventional financial performance criteria, namely, return on investment and return on sales, were clearly the most popular parameters for evaluation purposes. Conformance to planned objectives ranked second, and a variety of other less commonly utilized factors were reported. Our research found that for three-fourths of the companies surveyed, the volume of profits was the principal criterion used by home offices to evaluate the performance of their Brazilian subsidiaries. In many cases, however, profit volume was one of several criteria related to profitability. For example, return on invested capital was used by 31 percent of the companies, growth in profits by 27 percent, return on assets by 16 percent, and amount of repatriated· profits by 15 percent.

Besides profitability, many companies in our study reported that their home offices were also interested in the sales performance of their subsidiaries. Thirty-two percent of the companies considered growth in sales as an important criterion, 31 percent considered the amount of sales, and 24 percent evaluated market share performance. Other criteria, including such factors as productivity gains, control of expenses, and personnel development, were considered by about 20 percent of the companies surveyed.

[11] The Conference Board, *Measuring the Profitability of Foreign Operations*, Managing International Business Report No. 7, New York: The Conference Board, 1970.

Although European and Japanese firms seemed to emphasize sales performance more than the Americans, nationality in general played a relatively minor role in the choice of criteria. The Japanese concern about sales volume was partly prompted by the need to build recognition and position in the market. One Japanese manager remarked: "For the first five years our performance evaluation is based on whether we capture X percent of the market. After reaching this goal, the home office demands profits."

Executives in European companies tended to mention a larger number of evaluative criteria than their counterparts in Japanese or American companies. Part of this distinction may be explained by the different ways managers view the planning process. In the chapter on planning, we noted that for almost one-half the American companies, the annual plan represented a commitment or target figure to be achieved. In these companies "making the budget" was a crucial criterion in the evaluation process. For Japanese and European companies the plan seldom took on this air of importance. European companies generally had less formalized planning systems and tended to emphasize planning more as a means of coordination, not as a "contract" or commitment. In American companies the plan itself becomes a means of control over the subsidiary, and it might therefore be argued that fewer explicit evaluative criteria are needed, so long as managers follow the plan. Since the Europeans and the Japanese typically adopt a less formal posture toward planning, it seems appropriate that home offices assess a broader range of criteria.

Currently used control criteria and possible causes for different control practices, the subjects we have discussed thus far, provide useful data from which to build a more normative perspective. Writing on the problem of assessing subsidiary performance, Robbins and Stobaugh take a strong stand against what they observed to be the current practice of evaluating foreign subsidiaries on precisely the same basis as domestic subsidiaries.[12] Over 95 percent of the home offices of multinational corporations in the survey reported this practice. We concur with many of their arguments, which we explore at length later in the chapter. Nonetheless, other findings discussed earlier suggest that the problem may be of a slightly different character than Robbins and Stobaugh imply. They argue for the use of the budget (plan) as the key standard for

---

[12]Robbins and Stobaugh, *op cit.,* p. 82.

performance evaluation, and this approach has many benefits. Yet, as seen in the chapter on planning, this practice is already fairly common in American multinationals, a finding confirmed in the Conference Board study.[13]

Difficulties arise with the approach, however. First, the content of a plan or budget may be highly or inappropriately constrained, such that all subsidiary plans must conform to standard financial criteria. In such cases, use of a budget or plan would not accomplish a shift in the philosophy of control. Second, as discussed in the planning chapter, many subsidiaries are not involved in very extensive or meaningful planning activities. The plans that exist are often budget or financial summaries, and at best have an operating rather than a strategic focus. Finally, although a plan can serve as the basis for steering control, yes/no controls, or postaction controls, use of the plan or budget as a control device introduces new problems, which we discuss later in the chapter.

We remain unconvinced, therefore, that use of the budget or plan per se will itself eliminate many of the problems involved in assessing subsidiary performance. Indeed, if the budget or plan is used inappropriately, the consequences could be detrimental to the interests of the company, particularly to its head office. All this practice does is to begin what is an undoubtedly important shift of focus, toward assessing the desirability and feasibility of the objectives embedded in the plan itself.

In our view the correct approach to developing standards by which to evaluate subsidiary performance differs little, if at all, from the procedure that should be utilized for any business unit within the worldwide company. Appropriate standards must be related to the objectives of the subsidiary, and these in turn must flow from careful development of plans and strategies. Thus, while the criteria themselves may be stated and discussed as something apart from the plan per se, if they do not result from the process of planning itself, it is rather unlikely that they will be suitable.

Although key trade-off decisions will be made in the case of particular subsidiaries, we believe there are major categories of objectives which should be evident in all evaluation schema. (Specific targets or operational objectives that must be developed are beyond the scope of a general treatise.) These categories are basically similar to those which might be used for domestic operations, with the addition of one category, as follows.

[13]The Conference Board, *op. cit.*

Profitability objectives
Sales and market position
Cash flows
Host country relations

In each category the evaluation process means we are interested not only in absolute levels of these indices, but also in measures of change, comparisons with past and planned performance, and projected trajectories, as well as a variety of ratios which might be computed. It is essential to remember, however, that any performance data are meaningful only in a *relative* sense, relative to domestic and international competition, relative to market opportunity (including growth rate),[14] and relative to past performance.

The next step is to recognize the need to develop consistency in the planning and control system. Since subunit and/or subsidiary plans within a company are assumed to vary in content with respect to such elements as objectives, strategies, and programs, regardless of whether or not management accepts the rationale we have developed in this chapter for the trajectory of objectives of a business unit over time, it must nonetheless follow that any system which imposes uniform performance demands across disaggregated planning units must exhibit inconsistency. Just as strategic business objectives should form the basis for the key steering controls, so should achievement versus those objectives, adjusted where necessary for unanticipated environmental change,[15] form the basis for the key postaction controls. Yet in many companies this consistency has not been attained. For our Brazilian data, for example, we tested for association between objectives and evaluative criteria for the following combinations:

Strategic Objective	Evaluation Criteria
Sales versus other	Level of sales revenue
	Sales growth
Market penetration versus other	Growth in market share
Profit versus other	Level of profits
	Growth in profits
	Return on invested capital

[14]J. M. Hulbert and N. E. Toy, "A Strategic Approach to Marketing Control," *Journal of Marketing*, Vol. 41 (April 1977), pp. 12–20.
[15]*Ibid.*

Among the six tests performed, only one significant relationship was observed — subsidiaries pursuing sales growth objectives showed some tendency to be evaluated on the achievement of these goals.[16] For each of the other tests, the null hypothesis of no relationship was accepted.

Although at first sight this result might seem surprising, we are convinced that such apparent inconsistency is not unusual. Even in their domestic operations, many companies have avowed an enlarged commitment to strategic planning without any accompanying modification in the structure of operating controls or managerial evaluation. It is, for example, extremely difficult to attempt to inculcate a desire to seek longer term profits in growth businesses through higher investment rates and lower current profitability if that operation is a profit center whose manager is evaluated and compensated on the basis of annual profit.

The crux of our argument is that issues of performance measurement, evaluation, and control cannot be approached in vacuo. They make sense only within the framework of comprehensive strategic planning, of the type generally accepted by some U.S. and European companies.[17] To these frameworks must be added a new dimension, however — the consideration of the host-country environment. Even though both academics and businessmen have pointed out the importance of such factors, companies have apparently been slow to incorporate them systematically into their planning and control systems. Perhaps curiously, the oil crisis and the ensuing economic turbulence may have done much to hasten change in the planning area,[18] because major companies are certainly becoming more circumspect and careful in their international planning.[19] Moreover, the payoff bribery investigations of the late seventies may also spur more systematic con-

[16]Using Fisher exact probability test, relationship significant at the $p < .10$ level. All relationships were tested using either Chi-square or the Fisher exact test. For more detail, see James M. Hulbert and William K. Brandt, "Formulating Objectives and Evaluating Performance in the Multinational Subsidiary," *op. cit.*

[17]See, for example, descriptions of planning activities at General Electric described in "Corporate Planning: Piercing Future Fog in the Executive Suite," *Business Week,* April 28, 1975, pp. 46–50, or Texas Instruments, described in *Business Week,* September 18, 1978, pp. 66–91.

[18]"Piercing Future Fog in the Executive Suite," *Business Week,* April 28, 1975, pp. 46–50.

[19]Presentation by Cliff Davis to the *Multinational Product Planning Workshop, Marketing Science Institute,* Boston, January 1976.

sideration of the host-country environment and host-country relations in the area of evaluation and control.

OPERATIONAL CONTROL MECHANISMS

Achieving effective control by some means is clearly essential to the coordination of activities in the firm. Despite this need, however, a comprehensive perspective on various control mechanisms is rare. To some extent this state of affairs results from functional specialization. Accountants and controllers tend to stress a financial view of control; lawyers, a legal perspective; marketers, a marketing view; and so on. Child, however, takes a broad structural perspective, one which provides a useful organizing framework.[20] He presents three basic choices:

- between centralization and delegation.
- between formalization and informality.
- between heavy and light supervisory emphasis.[21]

We use these distinctions to help organize our discussion of various control mechanisms, although some overlap is inevitable.

In our view the mechanisms by which control is exerted are as important as the criteria chosen for control purposes. These mechanisms vary in cost, effectiveness, and appropriateness, and choice among them should therefore be made carefully and ideally, on the basis of matching to the task at hand. In fact, while we see that task requirements do play a role, other factors, including cultural precedent and traditions, are also important influences on company practice. Thus, although there are clear — if hard to measure — economic consequences to both overly elaborate or unduly meager control procedures, cultural and organizational factors often lead to departures from what may otherwise appear to be the most desirable alternatives.

Quite apart from the factors of cultural and organizational predilection, however, the fundamental determinant of the minimum necessary control by head office, the lower bound, is the interrelatedness of company operations, either among subsidiaries themselves or among subsidiaries and the home office. Although this

[20]John Child, *Organization: A Guide to Problems and Practice,* London: Harper & Row, 1977.
[21]*Ibid.,* p. 119.

interdependence is naturally affected by budgeting and planning systems, technological and strategic factors are often key influences on interdependence and can create the most compelling arguments for central management and control. It has been argued that only by becoming truly multinational can a firm achieve maximum returns for its innovation,[22] and the obvious advantages of "buying low and selling high" are certainly more readily available to the multinational.[23]

We may conclude that many large companies are strongly motivated to increase the degree of integration of their international operations. However, the need for both communication and control stems directly from the need for integration or coordination,[24] which in turn depends upon (among other things) the extent of interdependence in the system. The more complex the system interdependence, the greater the amount of information that must be processed in order to enable coordination, and the more elaborate the systems of communications and control.[25] Thompson has distinguished three types of interdependence.

Pooled interdependence exists when each part of an organization renders a discrete contribution to the whole and each is supported by the whole. Interdependence exists in that unless each part performs adequately, the total organization is jeopardized; failure of any one can threaten the whole and thus the other parts.

Sequential subsumes pooled interdependence, but in addition, direct interdependence (among the parts) can be identified and the order of that interdependence can be specified. Thus the output of one part of the organization becomes input to another — the interdependence is in serial form, but asymmetric.

Reciprocal interdependence is the most complex of the three cases, and subsumes both pooled and sequential forms. Here, however, outputs of each part of the organization become inputs for the others. Each unit

---

[22]Stephen H. Hyman, *The International Operations of National Firms: A Study of Direct Foreign Investment* (Cambridge, Mass.: M.I.T. Press, 1976), pp. 25–29.

[23]The offshore activities of U.S. electronics and television set manufacturers provide good examples.

[24]P. Lawrence and J. Lorsch, *Organizations and Environment,* Cambridge, Mass.: Harvard University Press, 1967.

[25]This viewpoint is consistent with propositions advanced by Jay Galbraith, *Organizational Design,* Reading, Mass.: Addison-Wesley, 1977, and M. L. Tushman and D. A. Nadler, "Information Processing as an Integrating Concept in Organizational Design," *Academy of Management Review,* Vol. 3, No. 3 (July 1978), pp. 613–624.

involved is penetrated by the other, and there is reciprocity in the inter-dependence.[26]

As a company becomes more multinational, there is strong a priori support for the notion that its activities become more inter-dependent. It can be argued that this is a tautology, that what we mean by multinational is a company with globally integrated strat-egies and operations. Certainly the multinational company comes much closer to the model of a highly connected interdependent system than of a holding company. However, as the shift to global supply, production, financial, and marketing strategies occurs, sys-tem interdependency moves quickly from pooled to sequential and beyond. A global perspective necessitates that the system must ultimately achieve reciprocal interdependence, at least in some key respects.

We gain more insight into these issues if we separate the man-agement job into key components, the strategic and the operating. This breakdown[27] divides the job of management into two basic types of task: the strategic (sometimes called the planning) task — deciding what is to be done, and (2) the operating task — doing as well as possible what has been decided. If we view the multi-national as a company involved in formulating strategies on a global scale, it implies heavy reciprocal interdependence among subsidiaries and functions. As we noted in Chapter 4, strategic decisions involve making resource allocations, and these in turn necessitate such additional activities as information collection, in-formation sharing, consultation, negotiation, agreement achieve-ment, and conflict resolution.[28] These activities are reciprocally interdependent and necessitate heavy flows of communications. Since strategic decision making should be associated with plan development and approval, we would expect heavy communica-tion flows to be associated with planning activities, and, as noted in Chapter 3, this pattern was indeed observed, with mutual visit-ation becoming a key communications activity during the planning process.

[26]James D. Thompson, *Organizations in Action,* New York: McGraw-Hill, 1967.
[27]"Texas Instruments Shows U.S. Business How to Survive in the 1980s," *Business Week,* September 18, 1978, pp. 66–91.
[28]J. U. Farley, J. M. Hulbert, and D. Weinstein, "Price Setting and Volume Plan-ning by Two European Industrial Companies," Vol. 44, No. 1 (Winter 1980), pp. 46–54.

Later in the chapter we examine some of the influences on changing patterns of organizational control in the multinational. First, however, we look at control mechanisms and how they are used.

Communication Systems and Procedures

Communications, discussed more fully in the preceding chapter, is a key element in any control system. Not only is communication necessary to transfer the information needed to ensure control, but the frequency of communication can also be one indicator of the closeness of supervision. The more frequent the flow of information (through impersonal or personal channels), the easier it becomes for the home office to monitor the operations of its subsidiaries. Thus, while communications have many other purposes, they also permit the home office staff to question results and variances in a way that would not be possible in the absence of communications.

Impersonal communication is almost always supplemented by some form of personal contact. Mutual visitation is one form; regional and worldwide meetings are other means. Both activities can foster coordination and are probably more likely to be used when simpler and cheaper means (generally impersonal) are insufficient to achieve the necessary coordination, because of the complexity of interdependency.[29] As we mentioned in Chapter 5, however, American companies showed a much greater propensity for both personal and impersonal forms of communication, reflecting their particular management philosophies and organization structures as much as interdependency.

Organizational Structure

Classical structure, and in particular breadth versus height of the management hierarchy, is another important influence on control. For an organization of a given size, narrower spans of control result in "taller" hierarchies with fewer subordinates reporting to each superior. Whereas other variables such as technological complexity are also important, the taller hierarchy generally permits closer scrutiny of subordinate (or subsidiary) activities than does a "flatter" structure. Recall from the chapter on organization that the

[29]Galbraith, *op. cit.*

tallness of the hierarchy between chief executives of subsidiary and home office was one of the key factors distinguishing American companies from their Japanese or European counterparts.[30]

Our results indicate definite relationships among organization structure and control procedures. Table 2 clearly indicates that firms with direct reporting structures were the least formalized in procedures and documents and the most decentralized with respect to headquarters.[31] No major differences were observed between companies using international divisions and those with global organization structures.

Planning and Budgeting System

The planning system itself also plays a very important part in the control process. The use of standardized planning systems is increasingly common among multinationals, and as Table 2 indicates, three quarters of the companies in our Brazilian study used them. Furthermore, as the company increases the number of subsidiaries, the pressures to formalize by standardizing systems — and thus to simplify the control process — are even stronger (see Chapter 3). Plans thus developed often provide, as we have seen, the criteria used for performance evaluation. Indeed, among American multinationals this aspect is frequently seen as the key purpose of subsidiary planning, and the plan is often treated as a performance contract by both subsidiary and home office.

Not all multinationals, however, treat plans in this way. Plans vary, as seen in Chapter 3, in terms of variety, time horizon, depth, and specificity. European multinationals, for example, have traditionally relied on a personal control system, stressing the use of trusted, reliable home-country trained managers, rather than on formal planning and control systems. In addition, overemphasis on the plan as a control device introduces distortion into the planning process, a factor that vitiates the use of plans to coordinate geographically dispersed operations. These trade-offs are complex, and we discuss them in some detail later in the chapter.

[30]We should also note, however, that a "flatter" structure does not necessarily imply greater subsidiary autonomy, since it is possible to augment the capacity of a superior in a flat structure through provision of assistants and staff groups, models, computer assistance, management information systems and the like. See Galbraith, *op. cit.*

[31]Note that none of our measures are concerned with decentralization *within* the subsidiary, but concern the headquarters-subsidiary relationships only.

Table 2
Organization Structure, Formalization, and Decentralization

Organization Structure	Formalization Measures				Decentralization Measures	
	Mean Number of Regular Monthly Reports to Headquarters	Mean Number of Regular Monthly Reports from Headquarters	Percent Receiving Regular Evaluation of Reports Sent to Headquarters	Percent with Completely Standardized Planning System	Percent Perceiving High Level of Decision-Making Autonomy	Percent Authorized to Spend more than $5000 for Unbudgeted Capital Item
Direct reporting	4.2	0.5	0	60	70	57
International division	4.5	1.3	33	83	33	22
Global structure	5.0	1.7	22	79	58	29
Total	4.6	1.3	24	77	48	30

Use of Standardized Programs

As pointed out in Chapters 3 and 4, it is useful to distinguish between standardized planning systems and attempts to standardize strategies and programs — the content of plans. The former becomes necessary as the company expands the scope of its operations; the latter is a riskier step and should be carefully considered on a market-by-market and product-by-product basis. Our survey suggests that companies approached the idea of using standardized programs more selectively than had previously been posited.[32] Cost efficiencies can accrue from standardization through marketing research, copy development, point-of-purchase and other sales promotional expenditures, and the overall planning effort. Standardization of programs also facilitates home office control of subsidiary operations. Instead of pursuing diverse strategies and programs, subsidiary operations become more convergent, more comparable, and ultimately more susceptible to home office control.

Formal Authority Limits

The scalar principle of classical organizational theory suggests that the scope of managerial authority should be subject to hierarchically ordered limits. In foreign subsidiaries these limits are usually most visible in their circumscription of unbudgeted expenditures. In some companies these limits are extremely low — less than $1000; in others the subsidiary chief executive seems to have almost complete freedom in determining the amounts. In general, American subsidiaries reported lower limits, $5000 or less being quite common; European subsidiary chief executives normally had more latitude (see Table 3). Similar limitations also existed for salary decisions, although home offices usually retain an important role in key hiring decisions in subsidiaries. Specified authority limits are part of a general procedural emphasis which normally emerges as a company increases in size and complexity, and appear to be necessary components of the increasing formalization that comes with size.[33]

[32]W. K. Brandt and J. M. Hulbert, "Headquarters Guidance in Marketing Strategy in the Multinational Subsidiary," *Columbia Journal of World Business*, Vol. 12, No. 4 (Winter 1977), pp. 7–14.
[33]Child, *op. cit.*

Table 3

Budgetary Limits of Subsidiary Chief Executives, by Nationality of Company

	Percent of Nationality Group with Budget Limit					
Company Nationality	Less Than or Equal to $5000	$5000 – $49,999	$50,000 – $500,000	No Effective Limit	Total	*Number of Companies*
American	67%	23%	5%	5%	100%	21
European	27	9	41	23	100	22
Japanese	67	0	0	33	100	9
Percent of all companies	50%	13%	19%	17%	100%	52

Administrative Procedures Manuals

Together with prescribed limits to authority, manuals specifying how to deal with recurring problems are further evidence of formalization. Some subsidiary offices have such manuals, often running to hundreds of pages; others have none. Predictability and consistency of response to administrative problems is very important to the smooth functioning of an organization; yet the extent to which this goal can be achieved by the presence of lengthy procedures manuals is open to serious question.

Staffing Practices

Staffing policies are another element in the array of control mechanisms. Company practices vary widely, but here we observed a sharp demarcation between European and American practices. Although the practice is undergoing change, the traditional European preference is for a trained cadre of home office managers to run its overseas subsidiaries. These managers retain close and personal ties to top management at the home office, and the pattern of control in the subsidiary therefore often depends on the personal characteristics of the subsidiary chief executive and his immediate staff, who are generally citizens of the multinationals. Such a practice encourages a personal but centralized control system within the subsidiary; however, the formalization of typical American companies is absent.

In contrast, the staffing practices of American companies heavily stress the hiring of local nationals in top management positions. In our Brazil study, we found that 24 percent of chief operating executives in American companies were Brazilian, compared to 8 percent for European companies and none for the Japanese.[34]

A similar pattern was observed for other senior positions — directors of marketing, finance, administration, and manufacturing. American companies place less emphasis on the personal or company-man approach to control and far more on the impersonal or system-based approach. With a more formalized control system — emphasis on planning, frequent reporting, and personal visitation — there is less need to rely on carefully trained and loyal managers from the home office to run subsidiaries. The emphasis of American companies on *system* rather than *man* makes it much easier for them to employ local nationals.

PATTERNS OF ORGANIZATIONAL CONTROL

Despite our treatment of control mechanisms in a linear fashion, a more accurate analysis requires that they be considered in an integrated, holistic, control system. Several dimensions should be evaluated in reviewing a complete control system. Two of these were discussed in Chapter 3 — namely, degree of emphasis on people versus degree of emphasis on system. Other factors include the organizational climate sought by the multinational company, the extent to which the home office wishes to exert direct instead of indirect control over subsidiary decisions and operations, and the degree to which close coordination of worldwide operations is necessary and desirable.

First we examine the concept of centralization versus decentralization. Although the inadequacies of this particular conceptualization of the control problem are recognized,[35] the paradigm developed below yields useful insight into control patterns.

[34]Brandt and Hulbert, *A Empresa Multinacional no Brasil . . .* , *op. cit.* p. 45.
[35]W. K. Brandt, "Determinants and Effects of Structure in the Multinational Organization," Research Paper No. 136A, Graduate School of Business, Columbia University, 1978.

With a centralized approach the power to make decisions is restricted to managers at senior levels in the organization. Because decisions are made by a small group of managers at the top, the need for elaborate communications and control procedures is reduced. Policy guidelines for dealing with planning, budgeting, and reporting practices are less necessary, as is the need for an infrastructure of staff. Senior managers keep a close eye on operations and become directly involved when necessary.[36]

In contrast, bureaucratic controls permit the home office to use procedures and guidelines to maintain more indirect control over subsidiary actions. Lower level managers are delegated responsibility to make decisions only within carefully prescribed limits. Under such a system, planning, budgeting, and reporting procedures are well specified, and are generally consistent for most organizational subunits. More people are involved in decision-making processes — many with the control system itself. Senior level managers are free to intervene in decisions, but typically practice management by exception, becoming involved at the request of lower level managers or when limits or procedures are violated.[37]

These descriptions of centralization and bureaucratic control strategies can be used and measured in several ways. Our first application to multinational subsidiaries uses measures that correspond to a paradigm advanced by Rutenberg.[38] The operational measure corresponding to centralization was the number of personal visits to Brazil by home office executives, a surrogate for the extent to which the home office intervened directly into the affairs of the subsidiary. The measure of "bureaucratization" was the extent to which the subsidiary was required to plan in conformity with a standardized format developed by the home office.

Although control strategies in the real world are more complex than the dichotomous paradigm shown in Figure 1, it identifies four categories which correspond to the following real-world archetypes.

The behavior patterns observed for companies falling into cells I and III are most consistent with the basic concepts discussed above. Cell I typifies the centralized company and cell III the de-

[36]J. Child, "Strategies of Control and Organizational Behavior," *Administrative Science Quarterly*, Vol. 18 (1973), p. 3.
[37]*Ibid.*
[38]D. P. Rutenberg, "Organizational Archetypes of a Multinational Company," *Management Science*, Vol. 16, No. 6 (February 1970), pp. B337–B349.

(Centralization)	(Bureaucratization)	
Number of Personal Visits to Brazil	Use of Formal Standardized Planning Procedures	
	Less Formal	Very Formal
Many visits	I, Centralized	IV, Centralized bureaucracy
Few visits	II, Laissez-faire	III, Decentralized bureaucracy

FIGURE 1 Typology of Organizational Control Patterns

centralized firm, contrasted by their emphasis on personal and impersonal control systems, respectively. The control patterns of firms categorized in cells II and IV, however, appear to be inconsistent. The laissez-faire companies (cell II) appear to be without any form of control system, whereas the centralized bureaucracies (cell IV) probably suffer from control overkill. Nonetheless, each type of company represents an actual pattern of organizational control and reflects a specific approach to management of foreign subsidiaries.

Application to Brazilian Subsidiaries

For the subsidiaries studied in Brazil, the following distribution was observed.

Cell	Description	Number of Companies	Percent
I	Centralized	3	5%
II	Laissez-faire	11	19
III	Decentralized bureaucracy	29	49
IV	Centralized bureaucracy	16	27
		59	100%

On the basis of this classification, an analysis of differences in the means for each group was conducted on four dimensions.
- Worldwide sales of parent company
- Number of countries with manufacturing subsidiaries
- Sales of Brazilian company
- Nationality

The differences reported in Table 4 show a consistent pattern. The companies in cell I were the smallest in terms of number of subsidiaries, sales in Brazil, and worldwide sales. The laissez-faire com-

Table 4
Company Characteristics by Control Category

	Type			
	I	II	III	IV
			Decentralized	Centralized
Characteristic	Centralized	Laissez-faire	Bureaucracy	Bureaucracy
World sales[a]	$935	$1156	$3096	$6126
Number of foreign subsidiaries	8.5	12.2	19.4	29.7
Brazil sales	$ 25.3	$ 42.2	$ 92.6	$ 99.3
Nationality				
Percent American	0	9	31	75
Percent European	100	64	48	13
Percent Japanese	0	27	21	12
	100	100	100	100

[a]*1972 sales in millions of U.S. dollars.*

panies (II) were next biggest in size, followed by the decentralized bureaucracies (III) and the centralized bureaucracies (IV). Moreover, cell I companies were all European, cell II predominantly European, cell III a mixture, and cell IV primarily American.

It should be noted that the results of Table 4 are susceptible to a casual and chronological explanation. Consistent with previous research, size of the company is a major factor leading to formalization and use of bureaucratic control procedures. In this case worldwide sales and number of foreign subsidiaries are the driving force toward a standardized planning format. Perhaps a control strategy of centralization becomes feasible only in a smaller international company. As the company grows, the parent's apron strings must be severed. At this point the company is managed more or less as a holding company, leaving subsidiaries to the care of their own chief executives in what we termed the laissez-faire model. However, there is interdependence among subsidiaries and home office, even if it is limited to the management of cash flows. Again, with the increase in company size, planning becomes unwieldy if all subsidiaries are left to their own devices to develop plans. The information-processing problems posed by the absence of format standardization may be soluble with eight or even fifteen subsidiaries; but as the number increases, so do the pressures for more standardization, which in turn encourages a decentralized bureaucracy.

For many very large companies this step is not final. In fact, the term multinational might be better reserved for a company that plans its strategies on a worldwide basis. In this view there are many international companies but relatively few multinational or global companies. It is the global corporation which occupies cell IV and has received the somewhat unflattering label of centralized bureaucracy. But let us see why this should be so.

Planning and strategizing on a global basis necessitates a high degree of coordination or integration among home offices and subsidiaries. Labor and raw materials must be purchased where they can be obtained on the most favorable terms, components are made in a limited number of locations to capture scale economies, money is raised wherever terms are most favorable, and so on. No longer is it possible for a subsidiary chief executive to operate independently, seeking to maximize the subsidiary's profits or growth, for example; these interests are now secondary. Global optimization is now the name of the game, and interests of particular subsidiaries must be subordinated to those of the company as a whole. Evidently the coordination necessary to pursue these kinds of global strategies can occur only with a definite reassertion of central control. The system is now more tightly coupled (one of the less visible costs of a global management concept), so that a strike in one country may cause shortages that affect the entire corporation. Thus, the centralized bureaucracy — which requires the plans, reports, and information flows that are part of a bureaucratic control system — also needs active central management control to resolve the problems that occur in a tightly coupled system and to make allocation decisions which should be globally optimal.

DEVELOPING A SYSTEM FOR CONTROL AND EVALUATION

The analysis to this point makes it clear that there is no "one best way" of developing a control system. Because control is critically important, however, it is our view that the analysis and planning of appropriate control systems require much more attention than it now receives. In such analysis and planning certain key issues arise in every control system. The following discussion is organized around these key issues.

Guidelines in System Development

Use Flexibility in Choice of Targets.   In system development, controls and evaluation criteria should be flexible. The criteria chosen and the performance standards chosen for each criterion must be appropriate to the strategic mission facing the subsidiary or particular business units within the subsidiary. Although many American companies are beginning to appreciate the dangers of uniform performance objectives for their domestic operations,[39] many still use standardized goals across all or most of their overseas subsidiaries. This means that the company must develop a facility for planning, as opposed to a capacity for performing the elementary mathematics necessary to parcel out overall corporate sales or profit goals among foreign subsidiaries on a uniform or proportionate basis. Nor will the crude accounting skills necessary to project pro forma budgets suffice. Such budgets are not only capricious and meaningless, but their implications may even be detrimental to the performance of the business unit in question.

The categories of strategic objectives discussed earlier — volume or share, profitability, cash flow, and host-country relations — are central to the planning process. However, the specific targets within each category should be developed from the overall objectives established for the business.

Revise Plans When Necessary.   Most American companies are quite firmly committed to using plans as part of their evaluation and control system. However, they often fail to recognize the need to retain flexibility in the control process. Plans reflect a series of assumptions about environmental changes — competitive actions, policies of the host government, and other factors; and even where contingency plans are developed, only a limited number of scenarios are feasible. Thus, when actual performance is compared with planned targets, the evaluator must consider the unforeseen events that may have vitiated the assumptions under

---

[39]"Westinghouse Comes Home to Electricity," *Fortune,* August 1976, pp. 154–156.

which the plans were developed.[40] Ascertaining whether or not the unforeseen environmental events should have been anticipated is beyond the scope of the present discussion, yet the essential concept remains that plans established at the start of the planning period should not be indiscriminately applied as evaluation criteria at the end of the planning horizon.

Choose Appropriate Planning Horizon. Related to our comments on choice of appropriate objectives and targets is the issue of planning horizon. Perceptions of time are chronically different between cultures and play a role in increasing the extent of functional differentiation within an organization,[41] but these differences are no greater than those which frequently bedevil relationships between home office and subsidiary management. As one home office manager describes the problem: "When they want something no period (of time), is too short, but when we ask them for results, no period is long enough."

Although a number of factors, including communications difficulties, contribute to these problems, the basic conflict for control purposes is often due to excessive pressure for short-term results, in most instances from home offices but sometimes from subsidiary executives. If the objectives are appropriate, the result is a more highly pressurized working environment. If inappropriate, such pressures can be harmful to the company's interests. A common example is the pressure for immediate profits. If these pressures become intense too early in the life of a subsidiary or of one of its product lines, they can jeopardize its growth prospects and potential for longer term profits and profitability.

Match Control System and Desired Organizational Climate. Any control system must strike a delicate balance between reliance on personal and impersonal controls which is appropriate to the particular organization and its circumstances.[42] Consider the archetypes discussed in the preceding section. The organizational adjustments necessary to move from a type I cen-

---

[40]Hulbert and Toy, *op. cit.*
[41]Lawrence and Lorsch, *op cit.*
[42]C. Cammann and D. A. Nadler, "Fit Control Systems to Your Managerial Style," *Harvard Business Review,* Vol. 54, No. 1 (January–February 1976), pp. 65–72.

tralized control strategy to a type III decentralized bureaucracy are immense and require development of a considerable amount of software, management training, probably some personnel turnover, and perhaps complete reorganization.

It is important, therefore, to modify control systems carefully, and, if a new system is being redesigned, to be sure that it matches the existing organizational climate as well as possible. For example, we have contrasted approaches to control by the extent to which they rely on personal versus impersonal means. The traditional European approach to organizational control relies more on the personal aspects and less on the impersonal. Rapid change toward more impersonal controls might lead to undesired reactions from managers who feel that their company is losing faith in them. On the other hand, in the absence of impersonal controls, misplaced faith in people leaves room for fraud, despotism, or a variety of other problems. Also evident is the fact that festooning subsidiary operations with excessive bureaucratic controls is not only expensive, but also communicates the suspicion that subsidiary managers are not trusted, and this suspicion may in turn compound the mutual antipathy or hostility, which can impede subsidiary/home office relationships.

Relate Control Strategies to System Interdependency. Two kinds of system interdependency are important for present purposes. The first kind is inherent; it has occurred because inexorable technological, economic, geographic, or political factors do not afford any choice to the company, at least in the short run. For example, a primary metal producer may use up its domestic ore supply and thereby become dependent upon the operations of its overseas subsidiaries for ores for smelting. Or the capital costs of innovation in certain industries may be such that products must be standardized on a worldwide basis and sold in all possible markets; major civil aircraft programs or new jet engine developments are suitable examples.

In most companies there is also a considerable amount of what we might call discretionary interdependency — the extent of interdependence is modified by management decisions. The evolution of the global corporation has generally proceeded toward more interdependence, with greater need for coordination and central control. The major impetus for such changes has been economic, but there are costs associated with the change. Managers choosing to integrate their global operations should recognize that this will mean an increased role for central management, more elaborate and sophisticated planning and control systems, and in most instances difficult home office/subsidiary conflicts, at least until a new modus vivendi is found.

The Need to Maintain Balance

All control systems engender both intended and unintended consequences. As the control system becomes more rigorous, the unanticipated consequences tend to increase. Thus, although the costs of no control may be high, so may the costs of too much control. In our Brazilian study we found two examples of these problems.

Circumventing the Limit.   Setting a reasonable expenditure limit for subsidiary managers depends on a variety of factors: type of industry, subsidiary size, corporate philosophy, and type of decision, for example. It would be naive to advocate any particular figure for all companies. Nevertheless, if subsidiary managers feel that the limit is too low or that home office managers will not listen to reason, they sometimes practice what is known as "limit avoidance." Using such a guise, a manager faced with a discretionary limit of $5000 who wishes to make a larger expenditure simply records the expenditure in two, three, or more components, each below the mandatory limit. Although this kind of avoidance is better than complete concealment and although good auditing should detect such behavior, the more important question is to ask whether the limit is appropriate or reasonable. For example, in a subsidiary with $50 million sales, a budget limit of $1000 or less for unbudgeted items hardly fits with the notion of decentralization, which the company espouses. Furthermore, such control policies are seldom reviewed, and given the explosive growth of some subsidiaries, these yes/no controls soon become outdated.

"Pressure Cooker" Problem.   In Chapter 3 we elaborated on the finding that for most American companies the plan represents a commitment instead of a coordinating device as used in other multinationals. If the pressure to meet these objectives becomes excessive, distortion is the inevitable result.[43] Budgets or plans, in a control context, provide standards for evaluation; however, they are not meant to be pressure devices. Finding themselves caught in such "pressure cooker" situations, subsidiary managers respond by doing everything possible to meet those targets. In simplest form, they resort to period-to-period manipulation of sales revenues and costs in order to "hit that bottom line," a practice openly admitted by several subsidiary executives whom we interviewed. More complex schemes completely conceal the true picture from the home office by preparing different sets of books — one for home office, often one for the government, and a third for subsidiary managers, which is used to run the local company. Such a response defeats the purpose of the corporate planning process. How much pressure should be applied to meet the planning targets is not a simple question, but the dangers of too much pressure are becoming apparent for some multinationals.

SUMMARY

The issues involved in the evaluation and control of subsidiary performance are complex and far reaching in their implications. Our results and those of other studies suggest that there is considerable room for improvement in current practice. Many systems now in use emphasize the yes/no variety of controls, which are difficult to monitor, given the remoteness of subsidiaries from their home offices. Multinationals also focus on postaction controls, which tend to focus more on where to place the blame than on ways to improve future performance. More attention could usefully be paid to steering controls, especially with respect to appropriate strategic business objectives for the subsidiaries operations. In many cases, reconsideration of these guiding objectives could provide a sound basis for subsequent realignment of both yes/no and postaction controls, particularly where these elements of the control system are lagging the changing strategic circumstances of the subsidiary.

[43]See Gordon Shillinglaw, "Divisional Performance Review: An Extension of Budgetary Control," in C. S. Bonini, R. J. Jaedicke, and H. M. Wagner, *Management Controls: New Directions in Basic Research* (McGraw-Hill, 1964), pp. 149–163.

Our results also suggest the need for progressive change in control relationships between home offices and their subsidiaries. The emergence of global strategies and plans in some companies will require that more information be processed, and that more effective systems for processing that information be developed. In some companies the move toward global planning will mean reassertion of more centralized control, and the change is likely to be both slow and painful, especially for subsidiaries long accustomed to considerable autonomy. Better planning of changes in organization structure and control systems could help make these changes less difficult. In many companies the managers affected by such changes learn of them after the fact, sometimes by reading the company newspaper. The organizational changes have profound effects on the balances of power in the company — quite apart from their obvious influences on the company's overall business prospects.

To be "multi" national requires coordination among operations in different nation-states. Collaborative attitudes are a necessary prerequisite for such coordination, and more attention to planning for, and communicating the intent of, changes in structure and control systems facilitates these difficult transitions.

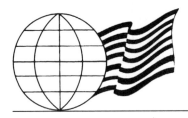

Chapter 7

Summary and Conclusions: Management Practice in Evolution

In Chapters 2–6 we described how subsidiaries of multinational corporations are being managed. Important management activities such as organizing, planning, communicating, controlling, and the choice of strategy were examined. In this final chapter we integrate our findings and summarize their implications.

Because nationality of the parent company seems to explain many differences we have observed, the first section presents a broad profile of management styles common to each nationality group — European, North American, and Japanese multinationals. Any attempt to draw comprehensive conclusions must be treated with caution, since no company can be labeled "typical" in all respects. Nonetheless, the similarities within and differences among nationality groups give reasonable validity to the general profiles.

In the second section we make some predictions about future changes in management practices of multinational corporations. For most firms the metamorphosis from a "national" company to an "international," "multinational," or "global" corporation is ongoing and far from complete. A number of trends and potential problems can, however, be identified from the evolutionary process.

In the final section, we review the implications of this evolution in the light of the current state of world economic development. In particular, we point out some of the basic reasons for conflict and disagreement between multinationals and their host countries, and indicate how these differences might be ameliorated.

NATIONALITY PROFILES: TRADITION DIES HARD

The European Mode

Most European companies were international long before the majority of American or Japanese corporations became international. Growth in the European companies, constrained by relatively small domestic markets, exerted inexorable pressures toward market expansion fairly early in their corporate lives. For some companies this expansion merely took the form of entrance into the markets of neighboring countries, through either exporting or foreign manufacturing. Other companies, particularly the Dutch and British, established vast colonial empires. Originally developed as sources of supply, these empires became increasingly attractive and important as markets for goods manufactured in the home country. Under the protection of a paternalistic colonial umbrella formed by home governments, these foreign ventures operated in a rather benign and managed environment, markets often characterized by preferential tariffs and limited competition. Consequently, although some European companies had acquired substantial foreign experience before World War II, the lessons learned were often inapplicable to the more internationally competitive conditions that prevail in many markets today.

This historical perspective helps to explain the management practices common to many European multinationals. In the early days home offices would send abroad managers or teams of managers with little direction or support. Communications and other linkages between home office and foreign managers were informal and infrequent. In effect, subsidiary managers acted as entrepreneurs on behalf of the parent company. In recent years, with foreign sales more important, markets more competitive, and technology more complex, such casual treatment of affiliates has become less and less possible. With such a long history of independence, however, moves to integrate worldwide operations naturally encounter resistance. From our survey, it is apparent that the struggle between the old and the new systems still continues.

Changes in organizational structure have occurred slowly in European companies. Only since the mid-sixties have many European companies begun to divisionalize in response to increased diversification and changes in their competitive environments.[1] Before the recent changes, most large European companies administered their operations through functional or holding company structures. The holding company structure embraced loose confederations of functionally organized subsidiaries, the central holding company usually doing little more than collecting and distributing dividends.[2]

Historically, most European companies have centralized decision-making power in the hands of a few top managers at the home offices and the foreign subsidiaries. Consequently, the organizational ties between headquarters and their subsidiaries remain relatively loose and unstructured. Because important decisions are made by top managers either at the home office or abroad, there is less need for an elaborate organizational hierarchy designed to decentralize responsibility and authority.

With this management philosophy, the need to advise, monitor, or control the foreign affiliate is reduced. The subsidiary manager is given wide latitude in which to operate, and as long as performance is maintained, the home office leaves him alone. Although all European companies do not permit such autonomy, managers in most subsidiaries surveyed receive greater decision-making authority, higher expenditure limits, and less intervention from the home office than their American and Japanese counterparts. They report to the home office less frequently and in turn receive fewer formal communications from headquarters. The same pattern holds for personal visits and conferences. In effect, some European subsidiaries still operate more as local entrepreneurial ventures than as integral units of a global corporation.

Long-range planning has been adopted comparatively recently by many European multinationals, and the problems of implementation are still apparent. Although managers recognize the need for longer range planning, the procedures still need to be developed. Compared with most American companies the plans

---

[1] Lawrence G. Franko, "The Move Towards Multidivisional Structure in European Organizations," *Administrative Science Quarterly,* December 1974, p. 493.
[2] *Ibid.*

of European firms tend to be less comprehensive, perhaps partly because the plans serve primarily a budgeting and coordinating purpose, not a commitment to performance.

Home office control over the foreign subsidiary is maintained by another means, namely the managers who run the subsidiary. In the absence of heavily structured management systems, many European multinationals rely on their centralized approach to funnel important decisions toward a few managers. Within the subsidiary, these managers are typically home country expatriates with substantial company experience. Often referred to as "company men," these managers are seasoned executives familiar with corporate philosophy and practice. Being so well seasoned, they require less direct guidance and monitoring from headquarters. In effect, the dominant presence of a company man supplants the need for a management system complete with plans, organization charts, voluminous reports, and policy manuals.

In our judgment, pressures are building to alter this traditional approach. Competition among enterprises, spurred by lower tariff barriers and economic alliances such as the European Common Market, has become increasingly global. The breakdown of cartels and other noncompetitive behavior, in addition to increases in the sheer size and complexity of the operations of European firms, is stimulating changes, in many cases propelling them toward similar approaches to those of the Americans, described below. We already noted the shift toward divisional structures, long common in American firms. Planning is also becoming more rigorous, as is the formalization of communications and procedures.

The evidence indicates that the days of relying only on the company man approach may be numbered. First, the supply of managers with the unique skills of the traditional company man simply does not equal the demand. Today, managers interested in foreign assignments have frequently received more years of formal education and even academic management training, but they are young and are without the decade of company seasoning so crucial to the European approach. Second, pressures are building in host countries to replace expatriate managers with nationals, a move complicated by the traditional approach. Furthermore, the staggering complexity and magnitude of international business today makes it less feasible to rely on the skills and efforts of a small cohesive group of managers. Their skills may complement, but cannot substitute for, modern management systems.

In summary, the European multinationals face a period of change, a transition that is likely to be painful. The historical traditions and precedents noted above have encouraged differentiation and independence among foreign subsidiaries. Executives accustomed to high degrees of authority and autonomy are invariably opposed to shifts toward integrating activities which tend to reduce their independence.[3]

In the early stages some European multinationals will lack the skill and systems to facilitate these changes; over time, however, there is no reason to expect that the transition will not occur. In the large mature European multinationals — Nestlé and Unilever, for example — these changes occurred long ago. In fact, the management systems of these companies are generally similar to those in the large American multinational.[4] The special conditions and history of the European company will mean that adaptation and evolution will not be identical to those of the American companies, but with increased formalization and integration, reliance on the company man will decline. This in turn should offer greater management opportunities for host-country nationals in European companies.

The American Mode

History, geography, and cultural values have also played a major role in the growth and development of North American multinationals. Blessed with a vast domestic market, most American companies saw little need to think seriously about foreign markets, except as a place to unload residual production.[5] Not until the late forties did the Americans generally begin the rush to Europe, often to establish assembly or full manufacturing facilities. Aside from mining and agricultural investments, major moves into Latin America and other areas did not begin until the late fifties and early sixties.

Managing the overseas growth created organizational difficul-

---

[3] Jack N. Behrman, *Some Patterns in the Rise of the Multinational Enterprise,* Research Paper No. 18 (Chapel Hill: The University of North Carolina, 1969), pp. 94–104.
[4] Kjell-Arne Ringbakk, "Multinational Planning and Strategy." Paper presented to the Academy of International Business, San Francisco, December 1974, p. 15.
[5] There are, of course, numerous exceptions to such sweeping generalizations — Singer, Gillette, and the oil companies being notable examples.

ties distinct from normal problems of coordination and control. Most American companies quickly grouped all foreign activity under an umbrella called the international division. North American cultural values demanded strict accountability, unity of command, a well-defined structure, and a management style that stressed the importance of a "system" or "way of doing things." The Europeans did not make similar demands.

As overseas business grew more important, companies responded with a more elaborate organizational structure. The management hierarchies became taller and more complex — until recently, when a reaction against such organizational complexity began a trend in the opposite direction.

Throughout this period the system for managing foreign subsidiaries became more institutionalized and formalized. Unlike the more personalized approach of the Europeans, the Americans have harnessed a system based on formal planning systems, policy guidelines, frequent reporting, authority limits, and numerous procedures.

These mechanisms are designed not only to support and monitor the operations but also to foster decentralized decision making. In theory at least, so long as the manager stays within the budget and obeys the rules, he enjoys the freedom of making decisions. For many American companies in our sample this promise of freedom is often a delusion. Although the mechanisms facilitate integration of worldwide operations, they also provide home offices with the means for controlling subsidiaries more tightly. As a result, the mechanisms listed above, in addition to frequent communications and visits from the home office, combine to give the manager less de facto autonomy than his European counterpart. Moreover, even when the American manager has the authority to make decisions, he shows a greater tendency to cover himself by first seeking home office approval.

The planning function, both short and long range, is well established in American companies. Problems still arise, but in contrast to the Europeans and Japanese, the major difficulties rest with implementation — getting managers at lower levels to participate and take the process seriously. The plan serves a very definite and serious purpose in American subsidiaries, namely, to specify a bottom-line figure for sales and profits that the subsidiary must achieve. The plan spells out how this should be accomplished, but the budgeted profit or sales goal becomes a commitment on which the subsidiary is evaluated. Although the formal planning system could permit a more flexible approach to performance evaluation, this practice was seldom observed in our survey. Indeed short-run profits were the primary, sometimes the only, criterion on which the subsidiary was evaluated.

Thus, in contrast to the Europeans, most American companies have developed a well-defined management system for coordinating and controlling their overseas operations. The problems with this system are its frequent rigidity and complexity. Some American companies run the risk of virtually drowning themselves in the morass of procedures and reports required even for routine decisions. This practice creates delays and inflexibilities, which reduce profits as well as morale.

One benefit of the American system is its ability to accept national managers in top foreign positions. Once the manager learns the "rule book" — the specified procedures and guidelines for various decisions — there is relatively little margin for error, particularly when the boss from the home office visits the subsidiary several times a year. We do not wish to give the impression that "learning the system" is an overnight exercise; yet, compared with the European approach, in which the manager learns the company philosophy through experience and word of mouth, the rule book approach is faster. This explains, for example, why IBM, which probably has one of the most sophisticated management systems, can rightly boast that nearly all overseas managers are host-country nationals. First, the manager is thoroughly indoctrinated with the IBM approach, often by working and training in the United States. Second, he is given responsibility within a well-specified set of limits; third, he is closely monitored and guided by the home office. Under these conditions IBM, and other firms like it, can take a chance with national managers, a step that many companies are still reluctant to take.

The Japanese Mode

Although leading Japanese corporations have a long history in international business, their involvement in overseas manufacturing is more recent. Until the late 1960s the Japanese developed most of their foreign markets through exports, generally in cooperation with large trading companies.

Only since about 1970 have the Japanese changed their approach to foreign markets by launching large-scale production facilities outside Southeast Asia. Brazil has received a major portion of this direct investment, and the Japanese now rank third, behind the United States and West Germany, in total funds invested in the country.

Such rapid and drastic shifts in strategy have caught many Japanese companies without the experience and expertise necessary to manage a world empire of overseas affiliates. In the past many firms relied on separate trading companies to handle their foreign sales; consequently, many Japanese manufacturing companies had little knowledge of foreign markets or how to develop them. While the trading companies concentrated on distribution, promotion, shipping, foreign exchange, sales contacts, and local-area knowledge, the industrial firms concerned themselves with production and technology.

Most of the Japanese companies in our sample seemed to be undergoing a painful period of learning and transition. Except for a few companies with long production experience in the country, most are relative newcomers, with all the problems of entering a market against well-entrenched competition. Because changes in strategy and procedures are occurring so rapidly, any picture depicting a Japanese style is likely to change before the paint is dry.

The Japanese organizational structure parallels the American preference in that nearly all companies use an international (overseas) division to handle foreign manufacturing and exports. The typical structure is not as tall and multitiered as in most American companies, but neither is it as flat and direct as in the European companies. Frequently, the overseas subsidiary continues to maintain its ties with the trading companies to obtain expertise, component parts, and other products to sell in Brazil.

The home office, which in some cases appears uncertain in its handling of the overseas affiliate, seems to maintain a rather rigid control over the subsidiary — most decisions of importance are referred to the home office. Communications between Tokyo and Brazil flow freely, but formal reporting in both directions remains in a state of continuous flux. In the meantime, personal visits serve as a surrogate and supplement to the reporting system.

Planning in the Japanese multinational corporation lags behind in quantity, time horizon, and sophistication of the plan prepared. Changes are occurring rapidly in this area, as many companies adopt what amounts to a one- and five-year planning system common to most American companies.

Influences of the Japanese culture leave a clear mark on the management styles of the Brazilian subsidiaries. Unlike many of their Occidental competitors, the Japanese seem to tip the balance of their objectives in favor of long-term growth and profits. Their marketing strategies support a willingness to forgo short-run profits if larger gains are possible in the future. For some of the more established companies in Brazil, their period of future profits has already arrived as they earn profits which surpass the average rates of their competitors.

In sum, the period of learning is creating significant changes and frustrations in the Japanese corporation as its executives struggle to build a system acceptable to both the Japanese and the local cultures. Until this system is developed, we expect that the top levels of subsidiary management will remain Japanese dominated. However, as demonstrated by the fact that some U.S. subsidiaries of Japanese multinationals are headed by Americans, changes are occurring which go beyond just window dressing and suggest that the truly "multinational" Japanese firm may yet evolve.

THE EMERGING GLOBAL ENTERPRISE

The nationality profiles just discussed are not intended to give the impression that the multinational as an institution has ceased to evolve. International companies have long played a central role in world commerce — trading companies such as the East India Company or Hudsons Bay are well known, but are probably not the earliest examples. The need to survive has required adaptation and evolution, a dynamic process that seems destined to continue. Since changes in strategy and structure are typically prompted by shifts in the environment, today's turbulent and uncertain environment suggests even faster changes in the future.

What does this process of evolution mean for the company engaged in international business? What changes can be expected for the multinational as we know it today? Although such predictions are notoriously unreliable, the results of our study offer some evidence of transitions that might be expected.

For many companies the quest for market opportunity has led to a state of "global overreach." They have embraced the view of a genuine world economy, what Drucker calls the "global shopping center."[6] However, this perspective has led to market prolif-

---

[6] Peter Drucker, *The Age of Discontinuity*. (New York: Harper & Row, 1969), Chapter 5.

eration, and many companies have not yet found the organizational structures and management systems appropriate for executing such strategies. Thus, many firms, although dynamic and aggressive in their marketing and financial decisions, have lagged in their internal development.

It is by no means unusual for changes in structure to follow strategic shifts; this phenomenon was observed repeatedly by Chandler in his epic study.[7] Recent research has suggested that the problem is now handled more normatively in domestic organizations,[8] but little theory or research is available to guide global companies in their development.

Behrman has suggested that centralized control and integration of subsidiaries are the key distinguishing attributes of a truly multinational corporation.[9] We have found, however, that many companies involved in foreign business are far removed from the model outlined by Behrman. Indeed, it should be made clear that companies do not have to be "multinational," with all the trappings this may entail. However, the opportunity costs of not becoming multinational are likely to increase. If integration of a company's worldwide operations really leads to the benefits claimed, competitors refusing to adapt may well find themselves at a disadvantage. Our own findings, although tentative, suggest that appropriate structures and management systems may be directly related to profitability.

If current trends continue, the firm's stamp of national origin will carry little meaning in the future.[10] More important will be the structure and system used to operate on a global scale. The archetypes presented in Chapter 6 — though that system is by no means the only way of classifying companies — suggest that the firms in the vanguard of the move toward global business are the

[7] Chandler, op. cit., p. 389.

[8] Richard P. Rumelt, *Strategy, Structure and Economic Performance,* Boston: Division of Research, Graduate School of Business, Harvard University, 1974.

[9] Behrman, *op. cit.,* p. xiv.

[10] Vernon projects that because home-country governments are becoming more restrained in their support of multinational activities, the multinational will have less motivation to maintain a close identification with the government of the parent company. "The world is my oyster" will be one step closer to the genuine policy of the enterprise. It is not accidental that several major multinationals are being denationalized in name. For example, British Petroleum is now BP; Badische-Analin Soda-Fabrik was renamed BASF. See Raymond Vernon, "Multinational Enterprise and National Security" in *The Economic and Political Consequences of Multinational Enterprise: An Anthology* (Boston: Division of Research, Graduate School of Business Administration, Harvard University, 1972), p. 121.

type IV companies, the centralized bureaucracies. They, more than any other type, epitomize the global or multinational corporation, as it is generally defined.

The systems and structures of such companies seem less and less likely to reflect an ethnocentric preference. Instead, they will reflect the requisites of the global job to be done. These companies are much better prepared to replace expatriate managers with nationals and to elevate them to top positions in the global hierarchy, a practice now observed in relatively few companies, though the practice seems to be increasing. These are also the companies most likely to permit and even seek increased local ownership — not just in one part of the world, but in many parts.

In strategy, too, we predict that vestigial influences of national identity on strategic choice may become a thing of the past. Product and manufacturing technologies, as well as worldwide competitive pressures, are likely to inhibit linkages between cultural precedent and strategic choice. In some industries the need for a tightly controlled worldwide strategy virtually compels tight control over subsidiaries, regardless of nationality.

Companies with global perspectives currently stand apart from their international competitors. Although size is partly responsible, the organizational responses to the challenge of creating global plans and strategies are also key factors.

Given the present state of the art, in theory and in practice, global optimization requires that key decisions on strategy and resource allocation be made centrally, generally at the home office. To make effective decisions, the home office needs substantial information about world markets. Foreign subsidiaries are key sources of these data, and planning systems serve to collect and present the information to home office decision makers.

Global optimization also implies that subsidiaries cannot be left alone to act in their own best interests, since these may not be consistent with the best interests of the whole corporation. Global optimization implies locating of plants to take advantage of favorable input costs, shipping costs, tariff barriers, host-country financial incentives, and a variety of other factors. Pricing decisions must consider tax and tariff implications; financing decisions involve currency fluctuations and varying costs of debt and equity capital. As a result the truly global company becomes much more of an interdependent system than its international precursor.

Whereas the decision to enter foreign markets may be seen as a logical extension of its marketing strategy, the development thrust of the global corporation focuses more closely on integrating its worldwide operations. In such a system the consequences of change or poor decisions at a subsidiary are not confined to that subsidiary alone; they can reverberate through other parts of the organization with multiplying effects. In this sense the multinational is a tightly coupled system, and the home office must do whatever it can to avoid such consequences. Hence we observe evidence of constant monitoring and involvement by the home offices, which frequently lead to various forms of direct intervention in subsidiary decisions.

In our judgment, to be multinational or global in the fullest sense requires the characteristics included in our definition of a centralized bureaucracy. As recently as ten years ago, such a control system might not have been feasible. Today, however, improvements in communications, transportation, and management systems, including the development of sophisticated planning and information systems brought about in part by the modern computer, have given rise to new possibilities. Does this mean that the wheel has turned, or will soon turn, a full 360 degrees? Have the type IV global corporations really become the centralized model illustrated by type I, where the home office dominates? We contend that companies have not returned and cannot return to such a system. The complexities of the type IV firms far surpass the ability of home offices to be omniscient. Rather, what is needed is the collaboration of home office and its subsidiaries in the execution of jointly agreed strategies.

The modus operandi for subsidiary and home office management in a type IV company, a centralized bureaucracy, is very different from that in other companies. Relationships must be cooperative and integrative, not characterized by the hostility sometimes expressed by subsidiary managers about "home office honchos." Creating such a spirit requires other changes. Overseas management positions cannot be filled by the maverick or freebooter, who feels confined by the domestic company or who subconsciously desires to become an entrepreneur, without risking his own capital. In the global corporation, relationships between home office and subsidiary managers should become more akin to those often found between corporate managers and the people running domestic divisions — not exactly free of disagreement, but not in open warfare either.

At the outset of this investigation, we hypothesized that nationality of the parent company would profoundly influence management practices and decisions at the subsidiary level. To a degree this hypothesis was confirmed by the results: nationality was an important explanatory variable. The more intriguing inference from the study, however, is that these nationality differences reflect a bygone era. Years may pass before companies operate without a national identity or without a keen consideration of home-country interests, but we foresee slow, inexorable movement in this direction.

THE CHALLENGE FOR THE DEVELOPING WORLD

Since the OPEC oil price increases of 1973, the economies of the developed countries have been mired in a period of slow growth. Companies in search of growth markets have been focusing their attention on the developing world. Spectacular changes have occurred in OPEC countries — real per capita gross domestic product in Iran and Saudi Arabia, for example, grew at an average annual rate of 7.4 percent and 9.8 percent, respectively, over the period 1970–1976. However, other developing countries have also fared well. Korea increased its real gross domestic product per capita at an average rate of 8.9 percent during the same period, and Brazilian overall economic growth recovered to 9.2 percent by 1976.[11] At the time of writing, even the economic prospects for such poor and populous countries as India and Egypt look brighter.

Thus, whereas the developing world is far from uniform with respect to its policies toward multinationals, the magnet of growth has meant that increasing attention has been directed by multinational management toward the less-developed and the developing countries. Yet, although some may argue that these efforts will produce net benefits for the host countries, the striking political vulnerabilities of multinationals are evident. With few exceptions, multinationals are creatures of the developed nations operating in the developing world.

From this perspective, it is as much in the interests of multinationals themselves as it is in the interests of their host countries that

[11] *1977 Statistical Yearbook,* Department of International Economic and Social Affairs, United Nations, New York, 1978.

a symbiotic modus vivendi be reached. In reality, foreign participation in the economy inevitably presents a mixed set of blessings to the host country, developed or less developed. Debating benefits and costs soon becomes a tiring exercise — in our opinion, it is more useful to try to identify the conditions that are likely to produce mutual benefit to multinational and host. Well-meaning attempts to develop codes of conduct for multinationals may help; however, since the problem is interactive, so is the solution, and codes of conduct for host countries are at least as important. Of course, sovereign nations will always wish to maintain their sovereignty, and any international code of conduct for multinationals seems likely to remain voluntary, but at the same time identification of conditions under which both companies and hosts prosper would be useful.

First, in our view, should be the necessity for host governments to organize effectively so as to deal with multinational firms. Not only does effective organization improve the host's bargaining power, but it also means that multinationals are more likely to be faced with coherent and consistent policies, rather than a welter of confusing laws and requirements.

The relative power of host governments to bargain with the multinationals is a concern of all developing nations.[12] Critics argue that the multinationals swing a heavy club when they bargain for concessions and other benefits. Examples of abuses of power can be found in any textbook or company history, but in our judgment the trend is away from such practices. Witness the recent furor in the United States and many other countries over the offering of bribes or excessive sales commissions to facilitate a sale.

The lack of bargaining power is generally due to two institutional weaknesses. The first is antiquated governmental structures — inadequate laws for levying and collecting taxes, controlling foreign business, or preventing the drain of finance capital.[13] The International Chamber of Commerce contends that many problems and misunderstandings would disappear if developing nations had well-constructed laws, efficient and independent auditing systems, fair tax structures, and effective labor laws.[14] An essential corollary to more laws is the need for effective administration of current and

---

[12] Richard J. Barnet and Ronald E. Müller, *Global Reach* (New York: Simon and Schuster, 1974), p. 137.

[13] *Ibid.*

[14] Richard Longworth, "Writing the Rule Book," *Saturday Review,* January 24, 1976, p. 24.

existing regulations. Brazil, where we collected our survey data, is superior to most developing nations in this regard, even though there is still room for improvement. Particularly in the area of antitrust and unfair competitive practices, various steps are needed to curb potential abuses of power.

A second problem identified by Barnet and Müller is the lack of a strong labor movement in most developing countries. They contend that with the exception of Argentina and Honduras, there is no labor movement in Latin America's manufacturing sector capable of effectively bargaining with global corporations.[15] This may overstate the situation in countries where the government plays a strong and relatively even-handed role in determining wage settlements and labor regulations, but the absence of organized labor groups does tip the balance in favor of the employer, whether multinational or domestic.

To derive maximum benefits from multinational participation in the economy may also require a certain kind of moderation in economic policy. Most firms, multinational or otherwise, loathe uncertainty. As the United Nations study points out, "a critical requirement of a multinational corporation is a reasonably stable environment in which growth and profitability are possible. Vacillating policy by host governments is perhaps as damaging as no policy at all, or even defective policy."[16] Thus managers are often more willing to trade off payment of higher costs (taxes, wages, social benefits, reduced incentives) as specified in government plans than to run the risk of not knowing what changes tomorrow might bring. In simple economic terms, multinationals are willing to accept lower profitability in return for greater stability in the business environment.

Some of the increased costs that multinationals might be willing to bear include the search for broader export markets and the eventual sharing of both hard and soft technology with domestic firms. The concept of technology sharing is a complex issue. Most attention typically focuses on the sharing of hard technology for advanced products or manufacturing processes, a sharing which occurs through licensing, franchising, joint ventures, or some other arrangement. Yet important benefits can also be gained through the transfer of soft technology, the systems and tools of modern

[15] Barnet and Müller, *op. cit.*, p. 138.
[16] *Multinational Corporations in World Development*, United Nations, New York, 1973, p. 83.

management. Soft technology provides the approaches and techniques for planning, organizing, controlling, training, developing strategy, and other management functions. For many multinationals this type of technology accounts for the major part of their competitive advantage. These companies have refined a management system that enables them to market products profitably throughout the world, even if the products and manufacturing technology are relatively standard. Manufacturers of many food and toiletry items fall into this category. These multinationals may have little hard technology to offer a developing country, but can provide valuable lessons to domestic firms in the form of planning, strategy formulation, and other tools of modern management.

Sharing this management technology with domestic firms can occur by design and by happenstance. In the crudest form, managers of domestic firms can simply monitor and study the behavior and practice of their multinational competitors. However, working for multinationals also provides excellent on-the-job experience which can later be applied in domestic firms. On a more formal basis, management contracts present an alternative whereby the multinational provides management services for a fee but without equity participation. Short-term training programs may also give practicing managers a quick, effective infusion of management skills and concepts. Equally important, however, are longer term courses in management education, which provide in-depth training for future managers. Finally, research findings such as those reported in this book can also facilitate the sharing of soft technology.

Besides the issue of technology transfer, there is also the question of who should own the foreign subsidiary. Host governments in developing nations increasingly believe that their long-run interests are best served by increased local ownership. In some countries, increased local participation is proceeding on a planned and gradual basis; in others the governments determine that immediate nationalization or sell-down is the best course.[17]

Although gradual increases in local ownership may be beneficial to the developing country, other factors should also be considered. For some companies and industries the multinational may have little to offer a developing country after a certain period, say

---

[17] A recent U.N. study found that nationalizations by developing countries doubled from an average of forty-five a year during the sixties to ninety-three annually in the seventies. Longworth, *Saturday Review, op. cit.,* p. 16.

twenty years or more. If a company's technology is standard, its products undifferentiated, and its management systems commonplace, the host country stands to gain little from foreign ownership.

For other companies and industries it is often preferable to avoid or limit local ownership, at least to the point of controlling the subsidiary. Industries relying on high technology, for example, are vibrant and are changing rapidly. To manage foreign subsidiaries in these industries, home offices require strict control and integration of operations. Local ownership and control of the subsidiaries in such cases may constrain the management process and may indeed limit the subsidiary's potential benefits to the host country. In summary, we contend that government programs to stimulate local ownership of multinationals should be selective and considerate of the benefits provided by the foreign company.

Governments should also evaluate the trade-off between investments in foreign subsidiaries and in domestic enterprises. With local participation, investors face the alternative of investing in a foreign subsidiary or in a domestic company. To the extent that equity capital is scarce — a common condition in developing countries — investment in the foreign company may indirectly stifle growth of the domestic firm. As a consequence, the capital-starved domestic firm may be forced to sell out or merge with foreign interests which can provide the needed resources. In effect, aggressive efforts to expand local equity participation in foreign companies may rebound to hurt domestic companies.

Instead of concern about the role of multinationals in their economies, many countries might be better advised to focus more attention on domestic enterprise. In many developing countries domestic firms are faced with the challenge of breaking out of the small-business syndrome characterized by family ownership and management. To obtain the capital, management expertise, and critical size necessary for this transition, many of these firms must eventually become public corporations.

It is to be hoped that, over time, greater mutual understanding will lead to responsive conditions being established and maintained by host countries, and to equally enlightened attitudes on the part of multinationals. Yet eventually the most satisfying outcome would be the emergence of more multinational companies based in the developing world. In the 1970s this trend accelerated. Brazilian and Korean construction companies were active in Africa and in the Middle East; oil companies of developing countries (often state owned) — Pemex, Petrobras, and Pertamina — extended exploration internationally; airlines such as Singapore Airways, Thai, and Varig were "sneaking" larger shares of international traffic; in shipping and fishing, traditional strong areas were further fortified.[18] Just as access to fast-growing markets is important to multinationals seeking growth, so is access to wealthy markets important to fledgling ventures seeking higher value added. Although the millennium may be distant, the trends are encouraging.

[18] David A. Heenan and Warren J. Keegan, "The Rise of Third World Multinationals," *Harvard Business Review,* Vol. 57, No. 1 (January–February 1979), pp. 101–109.

Appendix **A** — Chapter **2**

Organizing for Multinational Operations[1]

In Chapter 2 we reviewed some of the basic factors affecting organization structure. We identified nationality, size of foreign commitment, and relative size of subsidiary as having important effects on organizational structure. Although the chapter discussed most of these relationships bivariately, it is more appropriate to view the relationships multivariately and thus also to assess their relative importance.

DETERMINANTS OF VERTICAL SPAN

Table 1 reports the results of a stepwise multiple regression analysis which regressed the variables previously defined onto the vertical span of the organization.[2] The results demonstrate that even with the effects of size, foreign commitment, and other variables held constant, sociocultural differences still played an important role in the length of a firm's vertical span. Relative to American companies in the sample, European and Japanese multinationals

---

[1]The findings reported in this appendix appear in expanded form in William K. Brandt, "Determinants and Effects of Structural Design in the Multinational Organization." Research Paper No. 136A, Graduate School of Business, Columbia University, 1978.

[2]The stepwise procedure was terminated when the t value of the entering variable fell below 1.0. A preliminary analysis of variance to test for interaction effects between nationality and the other variables found no significant effects.

Table 1

Multiple Regression of Sociocultural, Parent Company, and Subsidiary Attributes on Vertical Span

Independent Variable[a]	Dependent Variable: Vertical Span	
	Standardized Beta	*t* value
Sociocultural		
European companies	−.26	2.34†
Japanese companies	−.31	3.02†
Parent-Company Attribute		
Percent of foreign sales (log)	−.34	2.59†
Number of foreign manufacturing subsidiaries (log)	.40	4.02†
High capital intensity	.40	4.15†
Textile industry	.19	2.34†
Office equipment industry	.18	2.27*
Subsidiary Attribute		
Annual sales (log)	−.25	2.54†
Sales/worldwide sales (log)	−.39	3.52†
Adjusted R^2	.74	
F value, d.f.	21.03†(8,47)	

[a]*American companies represent omitted value for nationality, medium capital intensity for technology, and motor vehicles for industry.*
*$p < .05$.   †$p < .01$.

operated through significantly fewer levels of formal hierarchy. The standardized beta coefficient for dummy independent variables should be interpreted as the relative difference from the excluded or base variable, in this case, American firms.

Among the parent company attributes examined, two of the size measures were statistically important. As the number of manufacturing subsidiaries increased, the complexities of dealing with more markets apparently created the need for additional levels in the organizational structure. Countering this tendency, however, were increases in the firm's proportion of foreign business, which operated to shorten the vertical span. It should be noted that these two characteristics, number of subsidiaries and percent of foreign business, behaved independently of each other ($r = .12$, $p > .10$), contrary to the belief that proportion of foreign business automatically rises as subsidiaries are established in more markets.

The countervailing effects of these two variables suggest interesting hypotheses for future research. That a firm tends to shorten its vertical span as it becomes more dependent on foreign business might imply a need or desire by headquarters to become more involved in the crucial strategic decisions affecting the subsidiary or the transfer of resources between subsidiaries. With larger numbers of subsidiaries, however, the operational autonomy of the subsidiary is likely to remain stable or perhaps to increase.

In terms of absolute sales volume, neither size of the world corporation nor its foreign sales had an important bearing on the vertical span.

Unlike the cross-tabular findings, which showed no association between vertical span and technology, the regression analysis indicates that more capital-intensive firms typically operated through longer vertical spans.[3]

Two of the four subsidiary attributes, absolute size and relative size, exhibited strong associations with the vertical span, in both cases acting to reduce the formal layering between headquarters and subsidiary. As a group the nine significant variables explained 74 percent of the variance in the dependent measure.

Determinants of Structural Design

To identify the key influences on structural design, a multiple discriminant analysis was conducted with the three structural categories (direct reporting, international division, and global structure) serving as the dependent measure.

Two significant functions were created to differentiate the three groups, the coefficients of which are reported in Table 2. The size of the standardized coefficients illustrates the variable's relative importance in each function. Although the structural design variable taps several dimensions of structure, seven of the nine significant variables were identical to those identified for the vertical span. The consistency of results across dependent measures suggests that at least several general determinants of organizational structure were isolated by the two analyses.

One indication of reliability is reported in Table 3, which shows that from the functions created by the discriminant analysis, 86 percent of the firms can be reclassified into the structural design actually used. This greatly exceeds the chance of probability of 38 percent.

[3]This result held for both measures of capital intensity and total assets employed/sales, as well as the subjective classification reported in Table 1.

Table 2

Multiple Discriminant Analysis of Sociocultural, Parent Company, and Subsidiary Attributes on Structural Design

Independent Variable[a]	Dependent Variable		Structural Design
			F value
	Function 1	Function 2	(final step)
Sociocultural			
European companies	.40[b]	.39	3.22†
Japanese companies	−.27	.16	1.46
Parent Company Attribute			
Percent of foreign sales (log)	.25	−1.14	6.69†
Number of foreign manufacturing subsidiaries (log)	−.45	.14	4.24†
High capital intensity	−.37	.01	3.50†
Pharmaceutical industry	−.31	−.07	2.35*
Office equipment industry	−.16	.39	2.03
Subsidiary Attribute			
Sales/worldwide sales (log)	.32	.98	8.36†
Years of manufacturing experience	−.03	−.65	3.03†
Canonical correlation	.80	.64	
Wilks Lambda	.22†	.59†	

[a]*American companies represent omitted value for nationality, medium capital intensity for technology, and motor vehicles for industry.*
[b]*Standardized coefficient.*
*$p < .05.$ †$p < .01.$

Table 3

Reclassification of Structural Group Membership from Coefficients of Discriminant Functions

Actual Group Membership	Predicted Group Membership of Discriminant Function		
	1	2	3
1 Direct reporting	8	0	1
2 International division	1	23	1
3 Global structure	1	3	12
Percent correctly reclassified — 86%			

Appendix **B** — Chapter **4**

Formulating Subsidiary Strategy

The results presented in Chapter 4 are partially based on some multivariate analysis, which is described in more detail in this appendix.

INFLUENCES ON CHOICE OF STRATEGIC OBJECTIVES

Table 1 reports the results of a series of multiple regressions that were run in an attempt to identify influences on choice of strategic objective. Although the results, discussed in Chapter 4, are in some ways disappointing, there is one particularly striking aspect to Table 1, namely, the key role of organization structure variables. With the exception of the findings that Japanese covpanies are clearly oriented toward sales growth objectives, all the other significant independent variables are measures of organization structure. Because of the absence of specific prior hypotheses, we should treat these results as only tentative. However, the relationships depicted in Table 1 and discussed in Chapter 4 are intuitively plausible, and are generally consistent with the strategy and structure arguments advanced by Chandler and Rumelt.[11] Though we

[1]A. D. Chandler, *Strategy and Structure,* Cambridge, Mass.: M.I.T. Press, 1962. Richard Rumelt, *Strategy, Structure and Economic Performance,* Boston: Harvard Business School Division of Research, 1974.

Table 1
Influences on Choice of Strategic Objectives*

Company Characteristics (Independent Variables)		Principal Marketing Objective (Dependent Variables)			
		Market Share (yes = 1)	Sales Growth (yes = 1)	Product/Market Diversification (yes = 1)	Profit Improvement (yes = 1)
Japanese company (yes = 1)	β†	−.25	.31	—	—
	t	(1.66)	(2.24)[b]	—	—
Company has internal market research department (yes = 1)	β	.35	−.16	−.31	—
	t	(2.44)[b]	(1.14)	(2.18)[b]	—
Company uses product managers (yes = 1)	β	−.31	—	—	.41
	t	(2.25)[b]	—	—	(3.09)[a]
Responsibility for new products assigned to marketing department (yes = 1)	β	—	—	.34	−.24
	t	—	—	(2.20)[b]	(1.82)[c]
Adjusted R^2		.29	.13	.13	.21
F (d.f.)		5.9(3,44)	3.3(2,45)	3.4(2,45)	5.8(2,45)
Significance		$p < .01$	$p < .05$	$p < .05$	$p < .01$

[a]$p < .01$,　　[b]$p < .05$,　　[c]$p < .10$ (two-tailed tests).
*The table reports a series of four dummy variable regressions, run with each major type of marketing objective as the dependent variable. Since the four objectives are mutually exclusive and collectively exhaustive, the regressions are not independent. However, the relationships noted above may be interpreted as convenient illustrations of the factors associated with different types of objectives.
†Standardized regression coefficient.

would hesitate to move from tentative description to prescription, the relationships in the table should also provoke some useful managerial pondering on the consistency of a subsidiary's strategic objectives and its organization structure.

EFFECT OF PARENT AND SUBSIDIARY CHARACTERISTICS ON EXTENT OF HOME OFFICE GUIDANCE

As noted in Chapter 4, we explored a variety of parent-company and subsidiary variables in an attempt to identify some of the factors associated with the extent of home office guidance. With respect to the "static" characteristics of parents and subsidiaries, the results were somewhat disappointing, as noted. In an attempt to extend the cross-classification analysis already described, we also used a step-by-step multiple regression procedure with the independent variables discussed above. The dependent variable measured the total number of categories in which guidance was received from headquarters. In this analysis the only variable demonstrating a notable effect was the presence of a marketing research department.

Failure to identify strong explanatory variables may be the result of one of several possibilities. First, perhaps the dependent variable did not measure the true extent of headquarters assistance. This was clearly a problem in previous research on the topic and is an area in which further work is needed.[2] Second, independent measures not included in this analysis may be the real driving force of headquarters guidance. Or third, there may be no one factor or set of factors that explains the use of standardized programs. Although we do believe that better quantitative explanation is possible, based on the findings that the only strong relationships found were those with respect to subsidiary strategic objectives (see Table 7 of Chapter 4), the third possibility seems very probable.

[2]R. J. Aylmer, "Who Makes Marketing Decisions in the Multinational Firm?" *Journal of Marketing,* Vol. 34 (October 1970), pp. 25–30.

Appendix C — Chapter 5

Managing the Communications Flow

In this appendix we examine research results dealing with the determinants of the pattern and volume of communication between home office and subsidiaries, home office understanding of subsidiary problems, and desires of the subsidiary chief executives for more information from the home office.

COMMUNICATION PATTERNS

Chapter 5 examined the interrelationships among various communication variables and found positive but weak correlations among different measures of both impersonal and personal communication. A factor analysis was conducted to search for dimensions other than personal and impersonal that might underline the data. The rotated factor loadings of the analysis are reported in Table 1.

Significant loadings on factor 1 refer to activities initiated or conducted by headquarters: visits to the subsidiary, evaluation of reports, and regularity of response to subsidiary reports. In contrast, factor 2 refers to activities initiated by the subsidiary, such as personal visits and reports to headquarters.

Factor 3 is loaded on two variables: frequency of regular reports to and from headquarters. Analysis as to why reports seem to

Table 1

Factor Analysis of Communication between Headquarters and Foreign Subsidiary

	Varimax Rotated Factors		
	1	2	3
Visits to headquarters	.03	.49	.00
Reports to headquarters	.11	.75	.45
Visits from headquarters	.41	.37	−.12
Headquarters evaluation of reports	.83	−.05	.17
Frequency of headquarters response	.56	.30	−.10
Reports from headquarters	.00	.02	.77
Corporate meetings	.05	.15	−.01
Total variance explained (percent)	29	19	16

emerge in a separate factor indicates that companies varied widely in their reporting practices but that this variation was not strongly related to other communication practices. Particularly at the home office, some firms operated on a management-by-exception basis, with very formalized reporting and evaluation systems at headquarters but infrequent response as long as no problems were observed. Other firms operating on an exception basis chose to deluge the subsidiary with frequent reports about political, economic, and competitive conditions. The subsidiary managers of some companies perceived this flurry of reports as a substitute for substantive help where and when it was really needed.[1]

The findings also suggest that various types of communication act as complements rather than substitutes. Although the informal communications network was not measured specifically, there is no evidence to suggest that where the formal system was inactive, the grapevine rushed in to fill the void. In such firms the findings indicate that there was simply an absence of communication between headquarters and subsidiary. At the other extreme, how-

[1]William K. Brandt and James M. Hulbert, "Communication Problems in the Multinational Corporation: The Subsidiary Viewpoint," *Proceedings of the American Marketing Association,* 1975, pp. 326–30.

ever, for some firms the communications system represented a fundamental mechanism to coordinate and control subsidiary activities.

DETERMINANTS OF COMMUNICATION PATTERNS

Although much research has been done on communication processes, there has been relatively little payoff in terms of understanding the determinants and effects of communication patterns in organizations. However, both theoretical[2] and empirical[3] efforts have been made to gain insight into the determinants of patterns of information processing and communications.

Our study attempted to identify key phenomenological attributes of the organization which bear on its communications system. The descriptor variables are divided into three groups: characteristics describing the parent company, those relevant to the subsidiary, and a measure of structural linkage between the two subunits. The criterion variables in the stepwise multiple regression models represent the factor scores of the two principal factors identified in Table 1. Factor 1 refers to headquarters-initiated communication and factor 2 to subsidiary communication.

Table 2 reports the dominant influences on each dependent measure. Communication from headquarters was significantly influenced by two attributes associated with the parent company: the number of foreign subsidiaries and the firm's level of capital intensity. More important than absolute size of corporate or foreign sales, the number of foreign manufacturing subsidiaries appears to be the driving force of the extent to which headquarters plays an active communications role. Two variables associated with the subsidiary — the length of manufacturing experience in Brazil and the presence of a Brazilian chief executive — accounted for a negative influence on communications initiated by headquarters.

National origin and size of the parent company were the dominant effects on subsidiary-initiated communications. Relative to

[2]Karl E. Weick, *The Social Psychology of Organizing*, Reading, Mass.: Addison-Wesley, 1969; and Jay Galbraith, *Designing Complex Organizations,* Reading, Mass.: Addison-Wesley, 1973.
[3]Andrew H. Van De Ven, Andre L. Delbeco, and Richard Koenig, Jr., "Determinants of Coordination Modes within Organizations," *American Sociological Review*, Vol. 41 (April 1976), pp. 322–38.

Table 2

Multiple Regression Analysis of Influence on the Communications System between Headquarters and Foreign Subsidiary

Independent Variable	Factor 1 [a] Headquarters-initiated Communication		Factor 2 Subsidiary-initiated Communication	
	Standardized Beta	t Value	Standardized Beta	t Value
Parent Company				
Attribute				
National origin:				
European			−.28	2.00*
Japanese			−.34	2.40*
Worldwide Sales			.26	2.02*
Number of foreign subsidiaries	.68	4.99*		
High capital intensity	.28	2.44*		
Subsidiary Attribute				
Years of manufacturing experience	−.43	3.22†		
National chief executive	−.32	2.72†		
Product diversification			−.20	1.58
Constant	.33		.50	
Adjusted R^2	.37		.26	
F value, d.f.	7.35†(4,51)		4.49†(4,51)	

[a] *Factor scores based on significant variables reported in Table 1.*
*$p < .05$.   †$p < .01$.

American firms, European and Japanese subsidiaries were less active in initiating communications. (The standardized beta coefficient for dummy variables should be interpreted as the relative difference from the excluded or base variable — in this case, American firms.) Absolute size of the parent corporation again encouraged a more subsidiary initiation, but in this equation the size of world sales was more important than the number of subsidiaries. The only subsidiary attribute to enter the model indicates that as product diversification of the subsidiary increased, subsidiary-initiated communications to headquarters declined. It is notable that none of the other subsidiary attributes — size, tenure, and type of chief executive — had an important bearing on the frequency of communications initiated by the subsidiary.

HOME OFFICE UNDERSTANDING

To diagnose the weaknesses of current practices we attempted to identify the factors responsible for effective communication. Accordingly, we built a multiple regression model to explain differences in how well the home office was perceived to understand subsidiary problems.[4]

The dependent variable in the regression was the subsidiary chief executive's opinion (measured on a five-point scale) of how well his company's home office understood his managerial problems at the subsidiary.

The results in Table 3 indicate that Japanese companies experienced the greatest difficulties with communications between headquarters and their foreign affiliates. Because foreign manufacturing is relatively new for the Japanese (outside Southeast Asia), many internal adjustments were still being made between headquarters and Brazilian affiliates to overcome communication problems. Subsidiary managers played down the problem of geographic distance, suggesting instead that cultural differences were the chief reasons for these problems.

Managers of capital-intensive subsidiaries reported better home office understanding. Because of the heavy capital investments required in these companies, planning, coordination, and home office involvement are frequently increased, which in turn should lead to better understanding.

Organization structure also influenced effective communications, although not in the way that might be anticipated. The type of structure, whether it was an international department or worldwide product divisions, had little impact on understanding. However, the complexity of subsidiary operations, as measured by the

[4]A more detailed description of this model is reported in William K. Brandt and James M. Hulbert, "Patterns of Communications in the Multinational Corporation: An Empirical Study," *Journal of International Business Studies,* Vol. 7, No. 1 (Spring 1976), pp. 57–64.

Table 3
*Multiple Regression Analysis of Home Office Understanding of Subsidiary Problems**

Independent Measures	Beta Value†	t Value
Company Demographics		
Japanese company (yes = 1)	−.45	4.10[a]
High capital intensity (yes = 1)	.20	1.84[c]
Organizational Structure		
Number divisions or major product		
lines in Brazil	−.26	2.34[c]
Reporting Procedures		
Amount information read		
by home office (1–5)	.28	2.64[a]
Number of monthly reports		
from home office	−.21	1.92[c]
Shared Experience		
Expert on Brazil at home office (yes = 1)	.29	2.67[b]
Years with company — subsidiary		
chief executive	.20	1.89[c]
Adjusted R^2	.52	
F(d.f.)	$7.36^a(7,47)$	

[a] $p < .001$,   [b] $p < .01$.   [c] $p < .05$ *(single-tailed test).*
The dependent variable measured the subsidiary chief executive's opinion of how well his home office understood his subsidiary's problems on a scale of 1 to 5.
†*The Beta value represents the standardized regression coefficient.*

number of divisions or major product lines, negatively influenced, home office understanding. As subsidiary operations become more complex, the tasks of coordinating and transmitting information, particularly at the home office, become more difficult and prone to bottlenecks and errors.

The formal reporting system also influenced understanding in an unexpected manner: the more reports sent from the head office to the subsidiary, the lower the perceived understanding. This relationship may be due to the type of information sent by the home offices, since some managers desired more information than others.

In contrast, the number of reports sent by a subsidiary to its home office shows no relationship to understanding. The use of these reports at headquarters is important, however. The subsidiary chief executive's opinion of home office understanding increases if he believes that his reports are being carefully read and evaluated.

Interpersonal relationships played a key role in the effectiveness of communications between headquarters and overseas affiliates. A home office superior who had worked in the Brazilian subsidiary or knew its operations well was believed to be an important asset to better understanding at headquarters. Similarly, the longer the chief executive's tenure with the company, the better the executive felt his problems were understood by home office.

DESIRE FOR MORE INFORMATION

Despite our conclusion that more information does not necessarily lead to better understanding, a substantial minority of subsidiary managers (31 percent) specifically complained that they did not receive enough help from headquarters. Much of the desired information was problem specific, such as product introduction, planning guidelines, control procedures, and so on. From the comments it becomes clear that some subsidiaries were largely forgotten or ignored until it was time for evaluation of their performances. In this section we attempt to identify the types of companies that desire more information or support from headquarters.

For the criterion variable in this model we found little theory or previous research to guide model development. Therefore, the approach was much more heuristic, and stepwise multiple regression with two-tailed tests was used to derive the equation shown in Table 4. Three variables indicated significant relationships with the desire for more information,[5] and each is now discussed.

[5]The following variables were tested, but were found to be unrelated to desire for more information from home office: Number of monthly reports from subsidiary to home office, number of monthly reports from home office to subsidiary, number of personal visits by the Brazilian executive to headquarters, number of personal visits to Brazil by home office superiors, use of regional or worldwide meetings, home office care in evaluating subsidiary reports, use of a standardized planning format for all subsidiaries, the subsidiary managers' tenure in Brazil or with the parent company, number of divisions or major product lines in Brazil, number of years subsidiary has been established in Brazil, type of organizational structure between headquarters and subsidiary, size of the parent company in terms of worldwide annual sales, proportion of worldwide sales outside home market, nationality of parent company.

Table 4
*Desire for More Information from Home Office**

Descriptor	Home Office Responds All the Time? (Yes = 1)	Brazilian Chief Executive (Yes = 1)	Low Capital Intensity? (Yes = 1)	R^2	F	Significance
Beta (standardized regression coefficient)	−.35	.40	.28	.21	3.39 (3,39)	$p < .05$
t value	2.04[a]	1.98[b]	1.92[b]			

[a]$p < .05$.   [b]$p < .10$ (two-tailed test).
*The dependent measure was a dummy variable coded 1 if the chief executive wanted more information, otherwise coded 0.

The extent of home office feedback to subsidiary reports varied greatly from company to company. Some responded every month regardless of need; others followed a policy of management by exception, responding only when a problem or opportunity was spotted; still others seldom or never responded to subsidiary reports. About two-thirds of the companies followed a practice of management by exception, but one in five (predominantly American firms) provided monthly feedback to guide and control subsidiary management.

Managers receiving regular feedback were much less likely to desire additional information when compared with companies in the other two categories. As one executive commented: "Home office doesn't always send the help we need, but we certainly don't want any more reports or guidelines; we can't read all that we receive now." Others noted that when the home office responds to every detail — a practice labeled "variance circling" by some executives — the feeling of being scrutinized can create an attitude of resentment toward any form of home office "intrusion," whether it is helpful or not. Thus, in some instances too much feedback can lead to resentment against requests for additional information, even where it might be needed by subsidiary management.

Subsidiaries with Brazilian chief executives were more inclined to desire additional information from headquarters. This finding may indicate that companies hiring nationals for top subsidiary positions find it more difficult to integrate the managers into the company system. It may also imply that the local manager is the real key to meeting the information needs of the subsidiary, not headquarters staff, which is supposedly charged with this responsibility. An expatriate manager with experience at the home office "knows the ropes" on how to obtain the needed information. A national manager often does not know parent operations as well as the expatriate and is thereby forced to rely on home office staff.

Subsidiaries requiring lower capital intensity were also more inclined to desire additional support from headquarters. This is particularly interesting when juxtaposed with the finding in Table 3 showing that subsidiaries with higher capital intensity had a better understanding with the home office. Most of the subsidiaries falling into the low capital intensity groups were producers of pharmaceuticals and consumer-packaged goods. As a group, these executives not only perceived that their home offices had less understanding of subsidiary problems, but also that they did not receive enough help in certain areas. Much of the information desired was marketing assistance. Several executives commented that they received little guidance for new products, and others complained about a positive bias in the information received. In the words of one manager: "We always hear about the 'winners' but we also need to know why the 'losers' failed in Venezuela or Argentina."

The Brazilian Survey
The companies and their managers

This appendix describes how the Brazilian study was conducted, and gives a profile of the executives interviewed and the companies they managed.

Although we were interested in a general perspective on subsidiary management, constraints of time and budget led us to focus on a single country of operations. Brazil offered a number of advantages for such a study. First, it is a large, single-country market with substantial foreign investment from North America, Europe, and Japan. Indeed, foreign firms have provided technology, investment, and skills critical to the development of Brazil, and today control nearly one-half the five hundred largest private companies in the country.[1] Further, companies from none of these areas could be said to be on "home ground" in Brazil — in this sense it is a neutral battleground. From 1965 to 1974, rapid economic growth, stable political climate, and government development policy combined to render Brazil unusually attractive to foreign firms looking for business opportunities. Although the higher oil prices and recessionary conditions of the mid-seventies have dealt severe blows to Brazil's growth, its population of 110 million, abundant agricultural and natural resources, and pragmatic development policies hold promise for continued long-term growth.

[1] William K. Brandt and James M. Hulbert, *A Empresa Multinacional no Brasil,* Rio de Janeiro: Zahar Editores, 1977.

COLLECTING THE INFORMATION

Company Selection

The sample of companies was selected in two stages; first the principal industries, then the firms within those industries. Six manufacturing industries were selected on the basis of three key criteria: (1) that they should be important sectors to the Brazilian economy; (2) that they should have heavy representation of multinational investment; and (3) that they represent a cross section of technologies as measured by degree of capital intensity. The three industries requiring heavy capital investment were motor vehicles and major parts (tires and motors), electrical equipment and telecommunications, and office equipment (computers and typewriters). The three industries requiring lower levels of capital intensity were represented by pharmaceuticals, textiles, and consumer-packaged goods (food and toiletries). In order to reduce the heterogeneity of the sample to some degree, mining and service industries were specifically excluded from the study.[2]

During the second stage of the sample selection we identified and contacted the largest foreign subsidiaries in each industry. In some industries — for example, motor vehicles — this meant that virtually all companies were interviewed. In others the largest three or four subsidiaries were contacted, followed by interviews with smaller competitors in order to balance the sample by nationality.

Interview Procedures

A total of 125 managers was interviewed at length about a series of management topics. The interviews were conducted first with the chief operating executive, and then, whenever possible, with the marketing managers of the subsidiaries.[3]

---

[2]Subsequent study suggests that many of the issues raised in manufacturing subsidiaries are applicable to the foreign operations of mining and service companies.

[3]In 63 companies, we met with the chief operating executive who was charged with top-management responsibility in Brazil. The remaining sixty-two interviews were conducted with high-ranking managers in the marketing department, generally the marketing manager. In 44 companies, we met first with the chief executive and subsequently with the marketing manager. In 19 companies, however, a second interview was not feasible; in these cases we chose firms of the same nationality and industry as the original chief executive interview and met with the marketing manager of the substitute firm.

The chief executive interviews covered the following broad topics:

- Planning conducted in Brazil and the involvement of the parent company in the process.
- The organizational links between the company and the home office.
- The kinds of communications flowing between Brazil and the home office.
- Controls imposed by the home office on the subsidiary.
- The decision-making freedom of the subsidiary's chief executive.
- Evaluation of the subsidiary by the home office.

The interviews with marketing managers focused on organizational issues, procedures for market forecasting and planning, development of marketing objectives and strategies, and measuring home office inputs into subsidiary marketing decisions.

In virtually all cases the executives interviewed were extremely cooperative and candid. To encourage this candor, each manager and company was promised confidentiality and anonymity in the publication of results. In addition to the interviews, other reliable sources, including publications and personal sources, were utilized to confirm and supplement the interview data.

COMPANY PROFILES[4]

Of the sixty-three chief executives interviewed, twenty-eight managed subsidiary companies with home offices in West Germany, Great Britain, France, Italy, Switzerland, Sweden, Finland, and the Netherlands. Because there were few companies in certain of these groups, they were combined and are referred to as European. Twenty-four companies were headquartered in the United States or Canada and are termed American companies; the remaining eleven were Japanese. Before grouping the European companies, a country-by-country analysis suggested that they could be combined without seriously biasing the conclusions.

More than 80 percent of the sixty-three companies were wholly owned, and all but one was more than 90 percent owned, by the parent company. American companies in the sample were most

[4]The discussions under Company Profiles and How the Companies Entered Brazil are based on interviews with only the 63 chief executives.

likely to be wholly owned (88 percent), followed by the Europeans (70 percent) and the Japanese (64 percent).[5]

Table 1 shows that the 1972 annual sales of the companies in Brazil ranged from $1 million to $725 million. Sales figures for American and European subsidiaries were almost identical with the median sales, being $54 million and $52 million, respectively. Japanese sales were much below these levels, with a median of $6 million.

Table 1
Sales of Participating Companies[a]

Nationality[b]	Sales of Brazilian Subsidiary (Millions U.S. $)		Worldwide Sales of Parent Company (millions U.S. $)	Overseas Sales as Proportion of World Sales[c]
	Median	Range	Median	Median
American	54	(5–350)	2600	26%
European	52	(1–725)	1300	67%
Japanese	6	(2–35)	1100	20%

[a]*In 1972.*
[b]American *includes companies headquartered in the United States and Canada.* European *includes West Germany, Great Britain, France, Italy, Switzerland, Sweden, Finland, and the Netherlands.*
[c]Overseas sales *include exports and overseas manufacturing, excluding intracompany transfers.*

Worldwide sales of the American multinationals were about twice the size of the Europeans and two and a half times the size of the Japanese. Thus, Brazil sales as a percentage of the company's worldwide sales were higher for the Europeans (3.6 percent) than for the Americans (2.1 percent) or Japanese (0.8 percent). Von Doellinger and Cavalcanti draw an insightful conclusion about these percentages. They note that although the multinationals are very important to Brazil's economy, the relationship is somewhat asymmetric. For all but a few multinationals, operations in Brazil represent only a small part of their global business.[6]

The European parent companies in the sample were, on average, more "international," in the sense that a much larger share of

[5]Joint ventures were excluded wherever the lines of ownership or managerial control were unclear.
[6]Carlos Von Doellinger and Leonardo C. Cavalcanti, *Empresas Multinacionalis no Industoria Brasileira,* Rio de Janeiro: IPEA/INPES, 1975.

worldwide sales came from outside the home market. Considering the relatively small size of many domestic European markets, it was not surprising that the products constituting 67 percent of European world sales were either manufactured or exported outside the home market. This compared with 26 percent and 20 percent for American and Japanese companies, respectively. However, because American multinationals were so large compared with other nationalities, their average volume of overseas sales in absolute terms approached the overseas sales volume of the Europeans. In fact, the overseas volume of the largest American multinationals exceeded the total worldwide sales of many non-American companies.

A breakdown of the companies by industry group in Table 2 shows that 19 interviews were conducted with electrical and telecommunications firms, 14 with makers of motor vehicles and related components, 11 with pharmaceutical and chemical companies, 11 with manufacturers of consumer-packaged goods, 5 with office equipment companies, and 3 with textile firms. The sample of European and American subsidiaries was drawn rather evenly from all industries except textiles, and are thus relatively comparable on an industry basis. Because overseas manufacturing by Japanese multinationals is still at an early stage compared with the Americans and the Europeans, most of the companies interviewed are concentrated in the electrical and telecommunications industry, in which the Japanese have historically been active and strong.

Generalizations from the Sample Results

Because our survey was based on a sample of multinational subsidiaries operating in Brazil and because sample selection was nonrandom, we must be careful in generalizing. We believe our results are fairly representative of the Brazilian situation, but extension to other host countries must be qualified.

Table 3 contains a series of size, performance, and financial measures for those companies in the Brazilian sample and for other multinationals which were not interviewed. The results show that in terms of annual sales and total company debt the companies interviewed were significantly larger than other foreign firms.[7]

[7]Because the sample included several of the ten largest companies in Brazil, some of which were *extremely* large, the means are heavily influenced by these few companies.

Table 2
Industry Classification of Participating Companies

Nationality	Consumer-Packaged Goods	Pharma-ceuticals and Chemicals	Motor Vehicles and Major Components	Electrical and Tele-communications	Office Equipment	Textiles	Total
American	4	5	6	7	2	0	24
European	5	6	7	6	3	1	28
Japanese	2	0	1	6	0	2	11
Total	11	11	14	19	5	3	63

Table 3

Size, Performance, and Financial Position of Multinational Subsidiaries: Companies Included in Sample versus Nonparticipants[a]

Company	Size Measures (in millions of cruzeiros)				Performance Measures[b]					Financial Position
	Annual Sales*	Profits Before Taxes	Equity Investment	Debt Investment*	Return on Assets	Return on Equity	Return on Sales	Asset Turnover		Total Debt/ Assets
Included in sample[c]	475	29.2	166	213	9.6%	18.8%	7.4%	1.26		53%
Not included in sample[d]	201	18.6	95	90	11.4	22.1	9.4	1.13		48

[a]Figures reported as medians.

[b]Return on assets includes profits before taxes divided by total assets employed: return on equity, profits/equity investment; and return on sales, profits/annual sales.

[c]Forty-five of the 63 companies whose chief executives were interviewed were listed among the leading 500 companies. The remaining 19 companies were not included in this analysis.

[d]These companies include 147 subsidiaries of American, European, and Japanese multinationals listed among the top 500 private companies but not included in the sample.

*Differences between means significant at p < .05 level.

SOURCE: Os Melhores e os Maiores, Sao Paulo: Editor Abril, Setembro 1974, pp. 16–34.

On the other hand, none of the other measures revealed differences which are statistically important.

From the comparisons in Table 3 we cannot draw conclusions about managerial practices, but the table suggests that apart from size the performance and financial structures of the companies interviewed did not differ markedly from other multinational subsidiaries in Brazil. Despite this reasonable similarity between the two groups, caution is still advised when drawing broad generalizations based on the sample.

HOW THE COMPANIES ENTERED BRAZIL

When They Arrived

Today, many of the leading multinationals in Brazil are mature, well-established companies with a long history of growth and progress. Among the companies interviewed, the Europeans came to the Brazilian market somewhat earlier than the Americans (see Table 4). The leaders of both groups came to Brazil before the turn of the century; nearly half established themselves in one form or another before the end of World War II.

Table 4
Date Manufacturing Began in Brazil, by Nationality

Nationality	Before 1946	1946– 1960	After 1960	Total	Number of Cases
American	50%	38%	12%	100%	24
European	37	48	15	100	27
Japanese	10	30	60	100	10
Overall proportion	38%	41%	21%	100%	61

The Japanese multinationals are more recent arrivals to Brazil: more than half of those interviewed entered Brazil after 1960. Although Brazil has received a major share of Japanese direct investment outside Southeast Asia, most of this investment has been quite recent.

Mode of Entry

Regardless of nationality, most companies originally came to Brazil to expand their markets for existing products. Some came for other reasons: to avoid tariff barriers, to integrate backward toward raw materials supplies, to take advantage of government and private incentives, and for one company interviewed, to take over a bankrupt customer.

Seventy percent of the subsidiaries started in Brazil as a sales venture, which later developed into manufacturing. This pattern was most common for companies requiring large capital expenditures — motor vehicles, electrical equipment, office equipment, and pharmaceuticals. Apparently these companies preferred to test the market first as a sales operation before committing larger sums of capital for manufacturing.

From Sales to Manufacturing

During the transition from a sales operation to manufacturing, more than 80 percent of the subsidiaries established their own facilities instead of acquiring a national firm. This finding does not support the frequent criticism that multinationals tend to enter new markets through acquisition rather than build their own facilities.[8] It should also be noted, however, that in many industries, when the multinationals entered Brazil, there were no local firms to acquire. Such industries as automobiles and electrical equipment and telecommunications were in fact created and developed by the investment of multinationals.

Although less than 20 percent of the firms in the survey had begun their Brazilian operations by acquiring a local firm, these same multinationals had accelerated the pace of acquisitions in the early seventies. These acquisitions were concentrated in the packaged-goods and pharmaceutical industries, but the nationality of the parent company had no relationship to the extent of acquisition on the part of already existing subsidiaries. Moreover, the discovery that relatively few subsidiaries entered the market by acquisition could be questionable, since the survey concentrated mainly on larger, more mature firms. Newfarmer and Mueller's

[8]A study of 1860 new manufacturing subsidiaries established by U.S. multinationals from 1960 to 1967 showed that 46 percent of the subsidiaries were acquired from local owners; see John Stopford and Louis T. Wells, *Managing the Multinational Enterprise* (New York: Basic Books, 1972), p. 147.

work indicates that more recent American entrants to Brazil were much more inclined to enter by acquisition of a local firm.[9]

Government policy may also affect rate of acquisition. Clearly, any policy restricting repatriation of profits tends to induce local reinvestment by multinationals. In many instances, such reinvestment occurs through acquisition of local companies, especially when this approach appears less risky than growth through internal diversification. Acquisition can frequently offer much-needed managerial talent and plant capacity, in addition to eliminating potential competition.

Although the Europeans as a group entered Brazil somewhat before the Americans, they waited longer before beginning to manufacture. The threat and aftermath of World War II certainly influenced this pattern more than Brazilian market conditions, because we find that nearly half the Europeans did not manufacture until the fifties (see Table 4).[10] Sixty percent of the Japanese firms did not begin manufacturing until quite recently — in the seventies for most companies. Among the industry groups, packaged goods and pharmaceuticals are the products manufactured earliest in Brazil.

WHO MANAGES THE COMPANIES

Chief Operating Executives

The average age of the chief executives we interviewed was forty-five; they averaged sixteen years of service with the company and three years tenure in their current position (Table 5). Although not shown in the table, the data indicate that intercompany mobility was highest among executives in American firms and lowest for the Japanese. Chief executives of Japanese firms had shorter tenures in their present posts, largely because of their companies' brief histories in Brazil.

[9]R. S. Newfarmer and W. F. Mueller, *Multinational Corporations in Brazil and Mexico: Structural Sources of Economic and Non-Economic Power* (Washington, D.C.: U.S. Senate, Subcommittee on Multinational Corporations, June 1975), p. 26.
[10]The timing of these investments coincides with global patterns in overseas investment. See Stefan H. Robock and Kenneth Simmonds, *International Business and Multinational Enterprises* (Homewood, Ill.: Richard D. Irwin, 1973), pp. 50–56.

Table 5
Backgrounds of Chief Executives Interviewed

Nationality of Parent Company	Years of Tenure			Prior Work Experience[a]		Field of Expertise			Number of Executives
	Age	With Company	As Chief Executive	In Brazil (percent yes)	In Latin America outside Brazil (percent yes)	Marketing and Sales	General Management	Finance and Accounting	
American	46	19	3.5	22%	67%	50%	25%	10%	21
European	43	16	3.2	25	33	42	42	8	25
Japanese	49	22	2.8	0	0	63	0	12	10
Average/total	45	16	3.0	20%	39%	48%	29%	10%	56

	Educational Background				
	Business	Engineering/ Science	Economics/ Law	Liberal Arts	No University Training
American	38%	19%	10%	24%	9%
European	17	29	29	8	17
Japanese	10	50	30	10	0
Average/total	24%	29%	22%	14%	11%

[a]Proportions include only expatriate (non-Brazilian) managers with previous work experience.

Despite their relative youth, the chief executives were seasoned and experienced managers, bringing to their jobs a breadth of experience acquired from former assignments. For example, two-thirds of the managers in American firms had worked elsewhere in Latin America; even the managers of Japanese firms — none of whom had prior work experience in Brazil or elsewhere in Latin America — had experience in other parts of the world, including Africa, North America, and Europe.

When asked to identify the one area of company operations where they felt most knowledgeable, 48 percent of the chief executives mentioned sales or marketing as their specialty area. Thirty percent considered themselves general managers, 10 percent, experts in finance or accounting. One moral seems clear: At the present time marketing seems the best background for a manager aspiring to be a chief executive in Brazil.

Finally, nearly 90 percent of the chief executives held a university degree. A business degree was more common among executives of American firms (38 percent), whereas a degree in economics or engineering was more commonly held by Japanese or European managers.

Marketing Managers

A comparison of Table 5 and Table 6 reveals that, compared with the chief executives, the top-level marketing positions were held by younger managers (41.5 years for marketing managers versus 45 years for chief executives) with substantially less company experience (7.9 versus 16 years) and less experience in their present position (1.9 versus 3 years). In fact, 30 percent of the marketing managers were less than thirty-five years old. Among the expatriates in this group, the Americans demonstrated greater breadth of experience; nearly half of them had worked in other parts of Latin America before coming to Brazil. The educational backgrounds of the marketing managers paralleled the chief executives' training, except for the higher incidence of business college degrees among the younger marketing personnel.

"Brazilianization"

We use the term Brazilianization to consider an issue of key importance to host nations around the world; namely, to what extent

Table 6
Backgrounds of Marketing Managers Interviewed

Nationality of Parent Company	Age	Years of Tenure		Prior Work Experience[a]			Educational Background				Number of Managers
		With Company	As Marketing Manager	In Brazil (percent yes)	In Latin America outside Brazil (percent yes)	Business	Engineering/ Technical	Social Science/ Liberal Arts	No Uni- versity		
American	41.2	7.0	1.7	33%	46%	34%	31%	21%	14%		29
European	42.5	9.9	2.0	22	25	44	30	22	4		25
Japanese	40.5	13.5	3.0	40	0	50	12	38	0		8
Average/Total	41.5	7.9	1.9	31%	32%	40%	29%	23%	8%		62

[a]*Includes only proportion of expatriate managers with previous work experience.*

are multinationals developing and employing nationals in top management positions? There are many dimensions to this issue, three of which are discussed below. Table 7 shows the proportions of chief executive, marketing manager, and top management positions held by nationals at the time of the survey.

The question of who really makes the big decisions is a sensitive issue in many companies — so delicate in fact that some rely on various charades to mask the fact that an expatriate still makes the decisions. For example, some companies engage a well-placed Brazilian and bestow the title of *presidente* or *director general* primarily for public relations and political purposes. Others may hire a national for the chief executive post but shift the effective power to the finance director or an "assistant to the president." Finally, in some multinational corporations, the power to make key decisions really rests with the home office rather than the subsidiary.

Table 7
Brazilianization of Company Managers

Nationality of Parent Company	Percentage of Companies with Brazilian Managers		
	Chief Operating Executive	Marketing Manager	All Top-Executive Positions[a]
American	24%	52%	56%
European	8	68	38
Japanese	0	13	16
Average	13%	53%	40%

[a]Ascertained by asking the total number of executive positions in the company and the number who were Brazilian citizens. Proportion represents the median.

Our chief executive interviewees were the top decision makers of the Brazilian subsidiary. American companies were far ahead of the Europeans or Japanese in employing Brazilian citizens in this position. Twenty-four percent of the American companies were headed by a Brazilian, compared with 8 percent for the Europeans and none for the Japanese. In fairness to the Europeans it should be pointed out that several managers came to Brazil in the nineteen forties — and fully intend to remain there — though they still retain a European passport and were therefore counted as European.

Over half the marketing manager positions were held by Brazilians. The European companies led the way here with a higher proportion of Brazilians, perhaps reflecting recognition of the need for Brazilianization and the desire to groom nationals for future top management posts. Remembering that marketing experience was the path to the top for nearly half the chief executives interviewed, we might see a higher proportion of Brazilians entering chief executive positions over the next few years.

Although we did not study other functional managers, it was evident that the financial or controller's responsibilities were generally held by expatriates. In fact, several managers commented that the controller's post would be held by an expatriate long after the chief executive position was turned over to a national.

Finally, the proportion of all executive positions filled by Brazilians shows that the Americans were again the most Brazilianized: 56 percent of all top management positions in American companies were held by Brazilians, compared with 38 percent for European companies and 16 percent for the Japanese. The European average is reduced to some extent by long-term residents who were still European citizens, but the statistical results are also supported by comments during the interviews. Several younger managers of European firms voiced concern about the need to incorporate more Brazilians in top management posts. One German executive warned: "We have to open up our company to the Brazilians; the days are gone when we can operate in a foreign land and ignore local concerns."

Nearly all managers reported plans to increase the role of Brazilians in managerial ranks, and from our observations the efforts generally seemed sincere. At the present time we feel that the American companies are perhaps best prepared for this shift, a conjecture supported by the above results and also by analysis of other data reported earlier in the book.

SUMMARY

The survey results derive from 125 personal interviews with chief operating executives and marketing managers of multinational companies in Brazil. The companies were selected from six major manufacturing industries, were somewhat larger than the average multinational subsidiary in Brazil, but were otherwise fairly representative.

The firms were headquartered in Europe, North America, and Japan, and annual sales in Brazil ranged from $1 million to $735 million. European companies had the largest proportion of world-wide sales outside their home market, but the total amount of worldwide sales of American firms averaged about twice those of Japanese or European companies.

Historically, European companies were among the early entrants into Brazil; the Japanese are the later arrivals. Most companies began as sales operations and expanded into manufacturing; the Americans tended to set up manufacturing facilities before the Europeans or the Japanese. Thus most multinationals we surveyed were mature, well-established companies with thirty or more years of tenure; many others, notably the Japanese, were recent arrivals having less than a decade of manufacturing experience.

Most chief executives were relatively young but well-seasoned managers, typically with a marketing background and a university education. Judging from the calibre of managers interviewed, it seems evident that the Brazilian market today is no longer a proving ground for would-be managers. The future for expatriate managers in Brazil is not bright, however, as more and more companies actively push to train and develop Brazilians for top-management positions. To date the American companies report the best overall record of Brazilianization.

Index